A Treasury of Farm and Ranch Humor

Copyright © 1989 by Lincoln-Herndon Press, Inc.

First Edition

Manufactured in the United States of America.

For information write to:
   The Lincoln-Herndon Press, Inc.
   818 S. Dirksen Parkway
   Springfield, Illinois 62703

Library of Congress Cataloguing in Publication Data.
Library of Congress Catalog Card Number: 88-082604
ISBN 0-942936-15-9

Write Your Own Jokes

Table of Contents

"I'm living within my means,
but I have to borrow money to do it."

Wait 'til Gran'pappy sees what the dang wind-storm did here . . . say . . . by the way . . . where is Gran'pappy?"

Introduction

It is strange that so few collections of farm and ranch humor exist. They are NOT to be found in the Illinois State Library, the Illinois Farm Bureau Library, or the University of Illinois Library, one of the largest in the United States. And it is passing strange to consider that, when the nation was young, 80% of the citizens were farmers and ranchers. Today, about 2% are farmers but the total population today is so much larger that we have nearly 2,158,800 farmers and ranchers not to mention those engaged in supplying the services needed on farm and ranch. Thus, there is a large, interested group of readers.

This lack is a puzzle. Perhaps past publishers felt that farmers were not readers of books and used literature for other purposes (remember those jokes about that special use of paper from Sears, Roebucks catalogues?). Or, perhaps they felt that only technical, "how-to" books on agriculture would be of interest to farmers. Or, perhaps the lack is due to the difference between country people since most of the people in the publishing business are city born and bred and, therefore, tend to think in urban terms.

It is certain that the lack of books of farm and ranch humor is not due to a lack of material. Most humor anthologies include a small section of country humor. And almost all farm magazines and newspapers carry at least a small section of jokes and cartoons. Further, it is a fact that since colonial days, farm and ranch jokes have been a major source of laughter for Americans in all walks of life. Witness the farm-based humor of Abraham Lincoln found in this farm and ranch treasury. And note the wonderful humor of the 1920s—also included herein. Clearly, farm and ranch humor is everywhere in abundance but, for some odd reason, few collections of it have been printed.

And it is for this reason that the Lincoln-Herndon Press offers A TREASURY OF FARM AND RANCH HUMOR to fit the need, interest, background and pocketbook of American farmers and ranchers.

And we interested a man of farm experience (the editor of this collection) with knowledge of cattle, hogs, sheep and most farm grains, who was a general farmer in the forties and fifties when most corn belt farmers were generalists. We think farmers, ranchers and all Americans will empathize, laugh and learn with the editor's selections that reveal the American farmer/rancher sense of humor, and his fun in the exchange of funny stories.

Almost 100 years ago, an English traveler wrote: "All over the land of America, men are eternally 'swapping stories' at bars and in the long, endless journeys by rail and steamer." And if he were writing today, we might add: "and at grain elevators, small town cafes, Farm Bureau and grange meetings — wherever farmers and ranchers meet." Country people enjoy swapping stories! For we are "a laughing people." And when life is hard, when weather or prices or bugs are against us, we laugh the hardest because that is when we need those healing stories and jokes that bring us laughter.

So here is the rural life of America revealed in its humor. It is suggested that you read it with your guard down and your spirits up, enjoying and understanding the wonderful, robust, hilarious humor that reveals rural life, and the way our farmers and ranchers look at that life in every generation.

It is further suggested that the reading be done in moderate doses. Like any delight, be it candy or apple pie . . . too much at one sitting can take all the joy and fun out of it. We need the chuckle because: "a chuckle is an antiscarecraft gun."

You will notice that following each joke or story, there will be a succinct, pithy folk phrase, saying or group of sayings. These remarkable vignettes come from all segments and sections of the nation. And they have been spoken by Americans from the 1870's until today. They represent the inventive comic genius for colorful yet precise language — words and phrases — spoken by John Q. Citizen.

These colorful sayings represent the poetic, imaginative, colorful and precise language of the common people in America, the farmers and ranchers and small town folk of this great nation.

Here you'll find none of the highly educated, low-key language typical of our genteel, British-oriented background. To the contrary, these words and phrases are *sui generis*—of, by and for the ordinary, hard-working, hard-playing, and hard-drinking American who makes out of native and imported ways of communication, a unique American language.

The people's talk is useful and always changing to meet new conditions. But our poetic genius for superb language invention remains up to the demand regardless of the changing conditions of our lives in our land.

The American language "as she is spoke!" is great fun...and useful.

John F. Kennedy said, "There are three things which are real: God, human folly and laughter. The first two are beyond our comprehension, so we must do what we can with the third." In the same vein, The Readers' Digest says, "He who laughs lasts."

Or, reduced to one word: ENJOY.

"Guess what I learned? If your gas tank reads 'half full', it takes only 8 gallons of water to make it 'full'!"

"Thought my boy might save you the trouble of making a trip out to the farm."

"If our topsoil is blowing away, whose topsoil is blowing in to replace it?"

Section 1

Contemporary Farm and Ranch Humor

"Mr Bookkeeper, I started out 40 years ago workin' for $1 a day—now you're showin' me my profit for the year . . . and I'm still workin' for $1 a day!"

"He calls it a 'Sire Data Base', but I call it a computer dating service!"

"Honey, some guy wants to rent our silo."

Two cows were grazing alongside a highway when a tank-truck of milk on its way to the distributor happened to pass by. On one side of the truck in big red letters was a sign which read, "Pasteurized, homogenized, standardized, vitamin A added, mineral rich."

One cow turned to the other and remarked, "Now that sure does make a body feel plumb inadequate, don't it?"

"Tell me Mabel, where did we go wrong?"

With permission of *Country Magazine*

That ol' boy was beef, beef plumb to the hocks.

The aspiring psychiatrists were attending their first examination on emotional extremes.

"Just to establish some parameters," said the professor, "Mr. Brown: What is the opposite of joy?"

"Sadness," said the student.

"And the opposite of depression, Ms. Elms?"

"Elation."

"How about the opposite of woe," the psychiatrist asked the farm boy.

"I believe that's giddyap."

It may seem odd—even unbelievable—but there is a

farmer in Colorado so fat he has his own zip code!

Up in Minnesota it got so cold one winter that the fire actually froze in the wood stove. They carried the frozen fire outside and parked it near the garage. The next spring that same fire thawed and burned the garage to the ground!

But that wasn't all. That same winter a feller came over and asked the farmer if he could marry his daughter. They were outside at the time, and the young man's words froze in the freezing wind so that the farmer never did know what the young fellow wanted.

The next spring the words thawed out, and the farmer heard the request, nodded approval and called the young man. But it was too late. Alas, he'd married another.

We was plumb certain the cook made the soup out of dirty socks.

An inspector with the USDA stopped at a southern farm and walked far out in the field to the farmer's cabin. "Looks like you grow about forty acres of cotton out here," the inspector remarked.

"Yup. That's right. And I got me the same number of acres in peanuts and corn."

"Well! You're a busy man."

"Yep."

"What time do you go to work?"

"Mister. I don't never go to work. I'm surrounded with it!"

They was close, thicker'n calfsplatter.

"Did you hear about the farmer who kept a rabbit in his house?"

"Nope. But why in the world would he want to do a thing like that?"

"He said it was an ingrown hair."

He was a short feller who looked like he'd been sawed off at the pockets. Why, he was so little they say he had to borrow a ladder to kick a grasshopper in the ankle! And he had to climb a box if he was of a mind to brag a little.

Then there was the Texas farmer who operated a roadside vegetable stand. A customer ordered one of his "Texas cucumbers."

"Texas cucumbers?" the puzzled farmer said. "Let's see now. What is it you want? Oh! One of these?" He held up a vegetable.

"Yeah. That's what I want."

"Mister," said the operator of the stand, "you got the wrong name for it. That's just a l'il ol' Texas string bean."

A farmer decided that the old ways of farming were finished. The new way was diversification. So he invented a hair restorer made out of farm products—corn, oats, wheat, soybeans, chicken feathers, goat hair, sheep wool, cattle horns and the like. It was enormously successful and he is now looking for investors. How successful was it?

Well, his hired man drank some and now has a hair lip! And his body grows so much hair he must be sheared twice a month. The hair is sold to the local mattress factory in such quantities that the hired man plans to retire in three years.

Experimenting, the farmer put some of his hair restorer on a worn-down broom and in one day the bristles were as long as the handle.

More! The farmer is elderly and uses a cane. He spilled some of his hair restorer on the handle and now he must shave that cane every morning before he can use it.

Now *that* is an innovative farmer.

I thought I'd never get in to see him. Took longer than an Oklahoma well rope.

A traveler through the southern Illinois oil-producing area, stopped to give a lift to a man. Curious about the area and the oil-rich farmers, the driver asked about the quick riches down there.

"Yeah," the farmer replied, "some of the folks down here got rich on them wells."

"And you, sir, were you among the lucky ones?"

"Yeah, I done all right. We got four good ones that'll make about 350 barrels a day."

"Really!" exclaimed the driver. "What in the world can you do with all that money?"

"I'm headin' for town right now," the farmer replied, "And I'm goin' to the real estate man and try to find me a farm that ain't got a lick of oil on it!"

When the shootin' started, them ol' boys come apilin' out of the saloon like ants out of a burnin' log.

A book agent stopped at a rich and prominent farmer's house. He offered a beautiful set of books on scientific farming. "It's a must for any modern, progressive farmer like you," the agent began but the farmer interrupted him after briefly reading the contents page.

"Can't use 'em, sonny."

"But why? With these you could farm twice as good as you do now."

"Likely, likely," said the farmer. "But I don't farm half as good as I know how now."

After I talked to him with my fist, he went along just as easy as a hoss-fly ridin' on a mule's ear.

The farm boy went to town to answer a "help wanted" advertisement for a house boy. He approached the mansion at the stated address, rang the bell, and an elderly woman came to the door.

"I came about your ad for a houseboy."

"Good. Would you mind wearing bermuda shorts?"

"No, ma'am."

"Let's see your ankles."

The farm boy hitched up his britches.

"They're neat enough. Now let's see your knees."

The farm boy hitched his britches higher.

"Well, I suppose you'll do fine. One thing more. Please show me your testimonials."

"Lady, I don't show them to no stranger, nohow. Goodbye!" And he turned and walked away.

"Acme Farm Supply? I'd like to place an order for a ton of steer manure . . ."

The only exercise he took was to bend his elbow lookin' up the neck of a bottle.

No water for me. Hell, I don't want to put the fire out.

Two farmers, one from Nebraska, the other from Iowa, were arguing about whose land was the most fertile.

"We grew a pumpkin so big," the Iowa farmer said, "that we ate three miles up in one of 'em and four miles down and five miles across and we never did know how far she went. We built a scaffold inside so we could eat it easier but I dropped my hammer. I went after it, fooled around all day lookin' for it when I met a man lookin' for his team of horses who'd got lost. He'd been huntin' them three weeks."

"That's pretty good soil you got," the Nebraska farmer said, "if you fertilize it properly—but it can't hold a candle to mine. Why my boys and I were out plantin' sweet corn. I was droppin' and the boys was hillin' it up. All at once the corn comes bustin' up out of the ground too fast so I had one of the boys sit on some of it. He did and the next day I had a note down from his sayin' 'passed through Heaven about noon yesterday. The angels really enjoyed our corn.' "

"That was rich ground all right," the Iowa farmer said. "You got any poor ground out in Nebraska?"

"Yeah, we got some—not much—but some where it's so poor it takes nine pheasants to holler Bob White!"

"Yeah, we got a smidgen of land like that in Iowa, only worse. The owner gave it to the church and they built a brand new church building on it. But, do you know, they had to spread four tons of fertilizer on it before they could raise a tune."

"Well drat my britches," said the ram, as he plunged from the cliff out into space, "I sure didn't see that ewe turn."

They tell the story about President Calvin Coolidge, a taciturn, abrupt President with no foolishness in him. One day he was asked whether the people in his state said, "this hen lays" or "this hen lies."

"In my area," Mr. Coolidge replied, "they lift her up and look!"

He was too slow and too late so that he got enough lead in him to melt down for bullets. And now he's takin' off his spurs at the pearly gates.

———————————

A farmer was enchanted by a side show at the county fair. There was an actual talking chicken and a talking dog. He rushed backstage and said to the owner: "I'll give you a thousand bucks for that chicken. Why, it's a genius."

"Naw. I wouldn't kid you or hornswaggle you. I'm an honest man. That old rooster can't really talk."

"But I *heard* him talk!"

"Naw. It can't. Just seemed that way. You see, that dog out there with the chicken, he's a ventriloquist."

———————————

Dangerous? Let me tell you this. That hog leg hangin' at his side shore warn't no watch charm.

———————————

Almost everyone suffered the heat and drought in the summer of 1988. Hens laid hard-boiled eggs. Some folks fried eggs on the sidewalk. It was told that in central Illinois, a man had to gargle soda pop before he could spit and the truest story of all told of this farmer lucky enough to grow a sound crop of corn. Unfortunately, it was so hot that the corn popped, floated up the fill the air like snow, whereupon the neighbor's beef cattle saw the white stuff, thought it was snow and froze to death.

———————————

He was a fast draw, was Junior. He could draw quicker'n you can spit and holler howdy.

———————————

A farmer in a Southern town was trying to decide what he ought to give his farm hand for Christmas, so he called him in and said, "Pete, you've worked real good for me this year and I want to give you a Christmas present that you will enjoy. Now which would suit you better, a ton of coal or a gallon of good drinkin' whisky?"

"Boss," said Pete, "I burn wood."

A farmhand was working hard and long, bucking bale for a cattle farmer in Indiana. After several days of it he went to the farmer and asked: "Boss have you got my name down proper—spelled right and all?"

"Sure, of course. Why do you ask?"

"Well, boss, I just want to be sure you spell it Simpson, not Samson."

He was so drunk he tried to hit the ground with his hat and couldn't.

A Basque shepherd, recently immigrated to the U.S., suffered a terrible winter with no pasture or feed. He went to the bank to borrow $5,000 and the banker put him through the mill, "You have security?"

"Si. You OK eet?"

"With a mortgage on your sheep, I'll do it. How many sheep you got?"

"One thousand!"

The loan was made.

It was a bitter winter and most flocks were lost or decimated and this caused the price of lamb and mutton to skyrocket. The Basque sold his sheep for $25,000, went to the bank and paid off his loan of $5,000. "Where are you going?" the banker asked.

"Back to my ranch."

"With all that money? That's dangerous."

"So what else can I do?"

"Leave it with me."

"How many sheep *you* got?"

Just that once he was too slow. The result was he got him a free halo and a ringside seat with them angels.

And there was the frugal farmer who informed the teller in the bank that he wanted to withdraw five dollars from his savings account. The snippy teller told him the minimum withdrawal was ten dollars.

"O.K. So I'll withdraw ten."

He got the money, then said, "Please mister teller, I'd now like to deposit five bucks in my savings account!"

Not all farmers are the astute, wise operators. There are a few like old Jake Jones from the Ozarks. He had two windmills but removed one because he said, there was too little wind to work both. He'd order seeds from last year's catalogues because directions said it took two years to bloom. He told about the heavy rain of 1972, how he saw an old hat floating down the road in front of his house. He tried to rescue it but a man was wearing it. "You all right?" he asked the fellow.

"Yep!" the man replied. "I'm settin' on top of the bales, but I'm worried about my son down there. He's drivin' the tractor pullin' the wagon."

"When you proposed to me, you DID promise
to lay the earth at my feet, BUT . . ."

With permission of *Country Magazine*

The last time I seen him he was goin' faster'n a cat with his tail on fire.

There's an ancient story that probably was first told by the Israelites emigrating from Egypt. It seems that a stranger asked a farmer if his son helped with the work. "Nope," replied the farmer. "He ain't home. He's in the city, a bootblack. . . ."

"Ah, I see," said the stranger, "you make hay while the son shines."

I hit him so hard on the jaw that he could scratch the back of his neck with his front teeth. And before I hit him he didn't have any teeth.

The farmer was window shopping in town, noticing the short and tight skirts on the models. Finally, he passed a traditional dress shop that had a sign in the window: "Ladies Ready-to-Wear."

"Well I should think so," he remarked, "it's about time!"

That man was so bald that when he took off his hat it looked like a full moon on the rise—or a baby's bottom.

He was givin' bed and board to a passel of crawlin', bitin' homesteaders.

Misrepresentation is not among the faults of the following advertisement written by Bill Nye:

"Owing to ill-health I will sell at my residence in township 19, range 18, according to government survey, one plush raspberry-colored cow, aged eight years. She is a good milker and is not afraid of the cows nor anything else. She is of undaunted courage, and gives milk frequently. To a man who does not fear death in any form she would be a great boon. She is very much attached to her house at present by means of a stay chain, but she will be sold to any one who will use her right. She is one-fourth shorthorn and three-fourths hyena. I will also throw in a double-barreled shotgun which goes with her. In May she generally goes away for a week or two and returns with a tall, red calf with wabbly legs. Her name is Rose. I would rather sell her to a non-resident."

It ain't far to Pyote, jest a jump, skip and holler away.

The Alabama farmer was having coffee at the town cafe. He announced to his friends, "Me and Priscilly are repairin' to go have us a little vacation."

"You mean you're preparing to go on vacation. To 'repair' means to fix somethin'."

"That's what I said," the farmer retorted. "Jest what I said . . . that we was fixin' to go."

He was cussin' like crazy, airin' his lungs real fine. His tongue was plumb frolicsome and his gab sounded like rain on a tin roof. But perty soon he shet up cause he'd run out of smart answers.

Everybody remembers the hot summer of 1988. That's the year a fox chased a rabbit and both were walking.

And a lot of farm folks fired the furnace to cool down the house so that the eggs stored there wouldn't spoil. But it really wasn't necessary because the hens laid hard-boiled eggs!

Busier'n a one-arm man holdin' a greased pig.

A certain man, living in a New England village, lost a horse one day, and, failing to find him, went down to the public square and offered a reward of five dollars to whoever could bring him back.

A half-witted fellow who heard the offer volunteered to discover the whereabouts of the horse, and sure enough, he returned in half an hour leading the animal by the bridle. The owner was surprised at the ease with which his half-witted friend had found the beast, and on passing the five dollars to him, he asked:

"Tell me, how did you find him?"

To which the other made answer:

"Wal, I thought to myself, where would I go it I wus a hoss; and I went there, and that's jist what he was."

Busy as a manure-loader based in a cow shed.

Two Northerners, traveling in the mountains of Kentucky, had gone for hours without seeing a sign of life. At last they came to a cabin in a clearing. The hogs lay in their dirt holes, the thin claybank mule grazed round and round in a circle to save the trouble of walking, and one lank man, whose clothes were the color of the claybank mule, leaned against a tree and let time roll by.

"How do you do?" said one of the Northerners.

"Howdy."

"Pleasant country."

The native shifted his quid and grunted.

"Lived here all your life?"

The native spat pensively in the dust. "Not yet," he said languidly.

I ain't sayin' it's impossible but it be kinda like tryin' to scratch yore ear with your elbow or huntin' fer a whisper in a big wind.

Did you hear about the hen that was never allowed to sit on and hatch her eggs? Well, one day it hailed big, egg-shaped balls of hail and that hen sat on them till she hatched out five penguins!

He prances out on the floor, squares off and stiff-legs it around in a sod-pawin', horn-tossin' mood and then sets to bellerin' like a newmade steer.

One year the wind blew so hard it took all the feathers off the hens. And their eggs came out scrambled. One farm wife was caught without necessary ballast and was blown flat against the wall so that all she could eat were pancakes and thin slices of cheese. She swallored a cherry by mistake and it almost exploded her!

And a boy missed his friend on the school bus. That evening he went to his friend's house and asked why he'd not been on the bus or in school that day.

"He'll be home in a few minutes, on the school bus."

"School bus! It's been here half an hour ago. He wasn't on it."

"Course not. The wind blew the boundary of the school district to the other side of our house. He's in a new district now."

E.B. White says that a farmer is a handy man with a sense of humus.

It was a town so tough the hooty owls all sang deep bass.

An Irishman, wishing to take a "homestead" and not knowing just how to go about it, sought information from a friend.

"Mike," he said, "you've taken a homestead an' I thought maybe ye could tell me th' law concernin' how to go about it."

"Well, Dennis, I don't remimber th' exact wordin' uv th' law, but I can give ye th' meanin' of it. Th' meanin' uv it is this: Th' Governmint is willin' to bet ye 160 acres uv land agin $14 thot ye can't live on it five years without starvin' t' death."

Farm relief: relieving the farmer of his farm.

A Texas rancher died and went to heaven. He rattled on the pearly gates and the doorman opened it a little and said:

"Well, all right, you may come in but after Texas, you won't like it."

An Eastern college graduate applied for work in a Michigan lumber camp. He was told to get busy on one end of a cross-saw, the other end being in charge of an old and experienced lumberman. At first all went well, but at the end of the second day the young man's strength began to wane. Suddenly the old man stopped the saw and spat.

"Sonny," he said, not unkindly, "I don't mind yer ridin' on this saw, but if it's jest the same to you I wish you'd keep yer feet off the ground."

"It's reserved for the first dollar I make farming . . . and it's been hanging for 15 years!"

That dude couldn't ride a board fence in a stiff breeze.

The sages of the general store were discussing the veracity of old Si Perkins when Uncle Bill Abbot ambled in.

"What do you think about it, Uncle Bill?" they asked him. "Would you call Si Perkins a liar?"

"Well," answered Uncle Bill slowly, as he thoughtfully studied the ceiling, "I don't know as I'd go so far as to call him a liar exactly, but I do know this much: when feedin' time comes, in order to get any response from his hogs, he has to get somebody else to call 'em for him."

The farmer had driven his team of mules to town and was late returning. "What took so long?" his wife asked.

"On the way back," he explained, "I picked up the parson and from then on them mules didn't understand a thing I said."

Dairy farmer, interviewing prospective hired man, "Have any bad habits—smoke, drink, eat margarine?"

A famous financier was taking a one-to-one, leisurely trip across the land. Curious about a fruit tree, he got out of his limousine, climbed the fence and moved toward the tree. A bull took after him and he barely made it to safety. The farmer-owner had watched the entire drama!

"That your bull?" the enraged financier yelled.

"Yep."

"The S.O.B. was chasing me!"

"Yep. I seen him."

"Is that all you can say? Hell, he might have killed me. And do you know who I am?"

"Nope."

"I'm the single most important cog in refinancing your state's debt!"

"Don't know why you're telling me all this. Tell the bull, he was the one chasing you."

That feller had more sand than the Gobi Desert.

A paratrooper landed in a tree, cut himself away from his harness and scrambled down into the farmer's pasture. Amazed and bemused the farmer watched the soldier walk toward him.

"Boy!" said the soldier, "That was a first for me."

"Me,too," drawled the farmer. "First time I ever did see a man climb down a tree without he first climbed up it."

A city man stops in a country store to buy a bottle of soda pop. As he starts to take a drink he looks over to the other side of the store and sees three farmers playing poker with a fox terrier.

He walks over to the game and stands there mesmerized as he watches the dog call for two cards, raise his bet, and rake in the pot.

Finally, the stranger says to one of the guys at the table, "That's amazing. I've never seen such a smart dog in all my life!"

One of the guys at the table looks up and says, "He ain't smart. Whenever he gets a real good hand he wags his tail!"

That old boy is so full of iron he'd rust if he stayed in one place very long.

An elderly farmer decided to take a vacation—his first in forty years—and go to Europe. His first stop was Spain where, upon the advice of the clerk at his hotel, he went to a fine restaurant for supper. He asks for the specialty of the house and he's served what looks like two large meat balls.

"What are they?" he asks.

"You eat—then I esplain," the waiter tells him.

It was delicious! He calls to the waiter and asks him what he had eaten.

"Eet ees from de bool. When he die in boolfight . . . the cajones . . . how you say, the balls. . . ."

The farmer was startled but recalling how good a meal it was he goes back the next night for another meal of it. And the next several nights the same, enjoying the food each night.

But one night the waiter brings his plate, a portion of two small, wrinkled lumps. After, he's finished them, he calls the waiter and asks why the meal was so inferior. "Lousy meal. Yuk! How come?"

The waiter shrugged and, with a quizzical expression said: "Sometimes ze bool, he ween!"

A gentleman farmer is one who has more hay in the bank than in the barn.

Them cattle was so poorly you could look right through 'em and read the brand on the off side.

A farmer was forced to listen to the boastful genealogy of a visitor whose ancestors had come over on the Mayflower.

"I'm from a very old family, my friend," said the visitor.

"So I hear," the patient farmer replied, "but in this business we know that the older the seed, the poorer the crop."

Quiet? Shore was. Yuh could hear daylight comin'. It was quiet as a thief in a henhouse.

A rancher attended his first church convention. Later, his pastor asked his judgment of the experience.

"Not bad. But I didn't understand why so much time was given to figure out how to get some people to come to church. When I attend a farm convention, they don't discuss such matters as how to get cows to come to the barn. They know that if a feller puts out good hay and enough of it, the cows will know where to come and get it."

It wasn't nothin' serious, jest a smallbore agrument.

He shore was successful, fer a time. Why, everybody around here figured his calves was havin' a calf a day the way his herd increased! But they finally caught him pinnin' crepe on another feller's calf. It wasn't that he rustled too much cattle, but that he was jest plumb careless about it.

A young farmer told his father that he was leaving the farm. "I'm off to the city, Pa. And I'm lookin' for adventure, excitement and wine, women and song. Don't try to stop me."

"Who's trying!" his father yelled after him. "I'm going with you!"

Busy as a one-armed paperhanger.

Talk about saving at the spigot and wastin' at the bung—why that boy'd chase a sparrow to hell fer the seeds in him and then spoil a danged good knife cuttin' him open.

A city fellow stopped his car near a farmstead and asked the farmer how far it was to Peoria. "Well," said the farmer. "If you continue the way you're headed it's about 25,000 miles. But if you turn around and drive the other way, it's 7 miles."

Busier than a one-armed monkey at a flea circus.

Illinos prairie is truly flat! They say that it's so flat that on a clear day you can see the bottom of a forty-foot well . . . if it's not more than ten miles away.

And when the wind blows it gets plenty dusty. The crows have to wear goggles and fly backwards to keep from choking on the gritty dust.

But Illinois isn't as bad as Oklahoma when it comes to drought. They said that when the Big Flood floated Noah, Oklahoma got only an inch of rain.

And Oklahoma is not as dry as Arizona where a rancher told a visitor that his father was seventy years old and had never seen rain. "I've seen it," this rancher said. "I was in

California once and it rained. Sure was wet stuff. But Pa never seen rain."

A year later, the visitor got a letter from the rancher who said his father had finally seen rain. It seems that on pasture one day, a tiny cloud sailed over and dumped about a cup of rain on the old man's bald head. The old boy was so shocked at this first-time experience that he fainted and his son had to throw a hatful of dust in his face to revive him.

"Artificial farm-fresh flavor added."

Definition of FARM: A four-letter word that signifies a hunk of land where, if you're up early enough of mornings and work sufficiently late at night, will make you rich—given two possibilities.

1. You strike oil on the farm.
2. You have a rich uncle who dies and leaves you $1,000,000.

Dried cow chips were a vital commodity on the range. They called them "prairie coal" and "compressed hay" when used for fuel.

A farmer was elected to his country Farm Bureau Board of

Directors. At the first meeting he scratched himself constantly. Finally, the farmer next to him turned and whispered:
"Why are you scratching like that?"

"Sh-h-h. Why? Because I'm the only one who knows where
I itch!"

You take a bedbug, he grazes and beds down. But a flea
ain't never satisfied.

"I hear you're not bothered anymore by your relatives coming to your farm every summer and then staying on and on,"
asked a friend.

"Nope. I learned that if I borrowed from my rich relatives
and loaned to my poor relatives, that not the one or the other
would ever come back to bother me."

They shore liked it there. They was happy as a flea in a
doghouse.

It is a known fact in Selma, Alabama that a farm family
nearby refused to allow their son to chew gum, explaining
that the sugar content of gum caused cavities. But they did
prepare for him bits of rubber cut from tires. This satisfied the
young man's craving and stopped tooth decay. The only trouble was that on his birthday and every year thereafter, he had
to have his teeth rotated and balanced.

That cowpoke came to town with a dirty shirt an' a dollar bill
and he didn't change either while he was here.

You may not believe it, but the tornados that struck Iowa
farmers in the summer of 1988 did over $10,000,000 worth
of improvements. Talk about pennies (dollars) from heaven!

He was a good young farmer, but in school he'd never

learned well the art of writing and spelling. So, when he went to the bank for a loan and they handed him a long form to fill out, he was uncertain. So he asked for help.

The first question was, "What are your parents' names?"

"Well," the young man replied, "I always call 'em Maw and Paw."

Colder'n a banker's smile.

In Arkansas they tell the story of the laziest man in the state who can be seen most any old day in a large oak tree fast asleep. Now that's not so unusual for Arkansas, but in this case, the fellow had laid himself down on an acorn—thirty years ago!

He never worked much but from the number of kids he's got he musta stayed right busy.

A flim-flam man offered shares in a venture of his own devising. He promoted his plan to cross the horsefly that lays 20,000 tiny eggs a season with the hen that lays big but only one egg a day, hoping to get a breed that would lay multiple eggs daily and all of suitable size for eating! But the plan failed for lack of faith on the part of inventors. Alas!

Now there's a new plan, this one would work with the manufacturers of Cheerios, that product to be used as seed stock for doughnuts! Makes sense!

No man ever pulled himself out of a hole with a corkscrew.

The pastor of the rural church drove by the farm of one of his members. He noticed the farmer in his hayfield baling hay.

"Brother, don't you know that the Creator made this world in six days and rested on the seventh?"

"Yep! I do know that," the farmer replied, worriedly looking up at gathering storm clouds. "But he got done with His work. Well, I ain't finished mine."

A farmer attended the Illinois State Fair, bringing his entire family. He was anxious to see the judging of Angus bulls, especially the Grand Champion.

But when he arrived at the exhibition tent, he found that it would cost over ten dollars for himself, his wife and ten kids. He appealed to the manager for a break, a lower price.

"Are all those kids yours?" the manager asked.

"Yes, sir!"

"Then you come on in free. All of you. I want that bull to see you!"

Big snake? Biggest snake I ever seen without the help of likker.

The United States has the greatest soils, the most productive farms and ranches, and the best operators in the world. Why, they say that in Nebraska, a farmer starts plowin' west in the spring and by mid-summer, he's ready to start back harvesting the crop all the way. And that's only an average farm! On the big ones they send a young married couple out to milk the cows and their children come back with the milk.

And corn! My, what a crop it makes. They store the corn in all outdoors and put what's left in the bins on the farms. (The authority for this last is Abraham Lincoln, the proof of which is in his very own, authentic tale in the chapter devoted to his farm stories!)

So when I figgers there jest ain't no way out, I starts askin' Saint Peter for a passport.

The mosquitoes are so big on Minnesota farms that the folks up there use mouse-traps to catch them. What do they use for bait? Mice! And they use bear traps to catch the mice.

He was brave—knew how to die standin' up.

"You been milking the cow with cold hands again?"

A farmer in Ohio was known for his money-pinching ways. And he hated to pay his doctor bills. So he treated himself.

This one time he not only had hemorrhoids that he treated with his nail clippers, but an earache. He simply had to see his doctor. So he did and was told to bring back a urine specimen.

"That old sawbones. Why does he need a urine sample when I've got an *earache*."

So he figured to fool the old doctor and collected urine from his wife, cajoled his dog for some drops, even got his grandmother to contribute, took the sample to the doctor and set back with an I'll-show-you-doc grin.

The doctor went to his lab and returned to report as follows:

"Your wife's got too much sugar, a mild diabetes, and your dog's got mange. Your Grandma is a bit anemic and if you don't quite using nail clippers on your hemorrhoids you're going to have one helluva 'n earache!"

How do you want yore eggs, Buster, dirty on both sides or both of 'em bright-eyed?

Jesse James and his gang once entered a railroad coach and announced: "Hands up, everybody. We plans to rob you gents and kiss all you ladies. So keep quiet and you won't get hurt."

One man stood and said: "It's OK to rob us gents but I'll be dadblamed if you-all are gonna kiss these ladies!"

An old maid said: "Now you hesh-up, mister. You jest let old Jesse go about his business. He knows what he's adoin'.'"

When he served coffee it was so thick that we used a fork to eat it.

During the war, farm labor was scarce and ranchers as well as farmers took what they could get. This one Arizona rancher hired a man who said he was experienced. After a few weeks a neighbor asked the rancher how he liked his new hand.

"He ain't a hand—he's a sore thumb!"

He had paper for backbone and was stuffed full of butter.

YOU CAN'T BE TOO CAREFUL ON THE FARM

A bunch of the fellers was settin around down at coffee and old John Jones was tellin' about his favorite horse, Birdy, when he and her hitched ready to plow and they was headed out to the field. Well, they come to his crick when old Birdy balked, first time ever. She jest wouldn't cross nohow! He led, he pushed, he begged but nothing worked. Finally, out of breath, old John got tired shovin' on old Birdy's rump and set down to have himself a smoke.

He sat down right behind Birdy, sighed, took out his pipe and matches, lit up and there come the most awful orange flash and explosion and old John was laid flat on his back and there was Birdy, clean across the crick, easy and grazing, calm as could be . . . Now it come about like this. Jest as old John lit his pipe, old Birdy let go one of her great big farts, even bigger'n usual from all the pushin and shovin old John and been adoin'. That fart caught fire and exploded from the lit match of old John. And that dern explosion come from Old John's match ameetin' Birdy's fart, head on, and the explosion set old John flat on his ass and blew Birdy acrost the crick. Birdy come off real good but old John had all the hair off'n one side singed off. He sure did look mighty funny.

In the farm community where I grew up, our undertaker was the most prosperous feller.

And that attitude puts one in mind of the gutsy old timer who advised his son, a beginning farmer, as follows: "You never know where your next break is coming from, son, and the best thing is to hope it won't be a compound fracture!"

That booze jockey served drinks that'd raise a blister on a rawhide boot. And he give a free snake with ever' drink.

Three cotton farmers were visiting at the cotton gin. They passed a jug of whisky back and forth for a time. Then, one remarked, "When I get paid for my cotton, I'm gonna get my wife the new stove she's been hankerin' for."

The second farmer took a long drink then said, "Soon as I

get my check I'm off to buy my woman a new sewin' machine she's been eyein' for a year."

The third farmer sat up and reached for the jug. "Believe I'd better have some more of this heah wishky cause I ain't out of debt yet!"

I like my whiskey strong enough to see double and feel single.

If you tell a Texan it's a nice, sunny day, he'll likely reply: "Shore is. And a few more like it'll ruin us."

It gets so dry around Pecos that they have to paper-clip stamps to letters.

Out there a traveler stopped to view a dry-blasted crop of corn. "Looks kind of short, don't it?" he inquired of the grower.

"Yep! She's shorter than when she was little."

It sure was scary to be throwed so high without wings.

On a dude ranch in west Texas, there was a sign in every bathroom:

No more than three inches of water in the tub. Out here we can't afford to spend water like money.

It was the kind of town where most of the doors swung both ways.

Many don't know, and more have forgotten that President Dwight D. Eisenhower was raised on a farm. He wasn't a great orator but he had this to say to the National Press Club conventioneers:

"It reminds me of my boyhood days on a Kansas farm," Ike related.

"An old farmer had a cow that we wanted to buy. We went over to visit him and asked about the cow's pedigree. The old farmer didn't know what pedigree meant, so we asked him about the cow's butterfat production. He told us that he hadn't any idea what it was. Finally we asked him if he knew how many pounds of milk the cow produced each year.

"The farmer shook his head and said: 'I don't know. But she's an honest cow and she'll give you all the milk she has!' "

"Well," The General concluded, "I'm like the cow; I'll give you everything I have."

He's a good feller . . . all heart above the waist and all guts below.

A long-winded visiting country preacher held forth lengthily to his country congregation. On and on he went interrupted by repeated pauses to slup down drinks of water.

An old farmer turned to his wife and whispered: "First time I ever saw a windmill run by water!"

She was as wrinkled as a burnt boot.

And a Sonora sheepman said he has bet three guys that it wouldn't rain ever again.

"Now that was dumb, George. You know you'll not win a bet like that!"

"That's what you think! Hell, two of them's paid me off already."

Watchin' him waddle down the street, you'd think walkin' was a lost art. He was so danged drunk that if you was to hold up a barrel with the end knocked out, he couldn't pour whiskey in it.

And then there's the tale of the first grade teacher who, in arithmetic, asked Tommy:

"If I lay one egg on this table and two on my chair here,

just how many will I have altogether?"

"Teacher," replied Tommy, "I jest don't think you're built right fer to do it."

ALLAN K. JENSEN

"Yeah, I'm making ends meet—
I just wish they would overlap a little bit!"

With permission of Country Magazine

I cain't help it if I et them deceitful beans as talk behind your back.

They say that the folks from Rackensach (an early name for Arkansas) are lazy. Here's why they say it:

A beautiful young bride screamed at her husband: "Ike! Yer beard is on fire. Do suthin! Do suthin!"

"I am Mary Lou," he yelled back. "Cain't y'all see me aprayin' hard as can be fer itta rain?"

Why, that meat was so tough I had to sharpen my knife to cut the gravy.

Little Oswald toddled out to the field where his Pa was plowing to report, "There's a strange man at the house. I dunno what he wants."

"Son," the father told him, "if it's the landlord, he wants his rent. If it's the banker, he's come to foreclose the mortgage. And if he's a traveling salesman, you run home fast as your legs will carry you—and sit in your maw's lap till I get there!"

The old cowboy said there was only two things he was afraid of. One, a decent woman; two, being' left afoot! And the worst of all is a widow of the grass variety. Ya can't stop 'em with a forty foot rope and a snubbin' post. They're goers. But if ya want flavor in yore grub, ya better go git ya one. Another good thing is they is always willin' to surrender same as a willow in the wind. And it don't matter if they got short ropes 'cause they shore throws wide loops.

It was a terribly dry year, nearly as bad as 1934 and dust bowl days. Two cowmen were discussing just how bad it was on their spreads. One of them sighed, took a long drink of coffee and said, "Well, I guess the good Lord'll send us rain jest as soon as we need it bad enough." The other cowman shook his head, saying, "If the Lord don't know we need lotsa rain right now, all I can say is . . . He's a damn pore cowman."

That old boy knows what to do with them critters. He's been on the cow's side of the fence, you can bet on that.

You can talk all you want to about tough guys, the modern Paul Bunyans', Pecos Bills' and John Henrys', but none of 'em can hold an anvil to this old Arizona superman:

Into the bar of a Texas whiskey mill walked a rough, tough, hairy and enormous stranger. He dragged a chained cougar after him and the wild beast growled and bit its chain then leaped for the tough guy who hit it with an iron fist, then kicked and beat the cougar to submission. Then old tough guy walked to the bar, ordered and drank rapidly five shots of whiskey.

But after the fourth shot, a rattlesnake poked its head from the guy's breast pocket, then rattled and thrashed and struck right and left. "That's enough out'n you, Gertrude. You git back where ya belong." And he whacked the snake into quiet submission and shoved it back into his breast pocket.

"Where you from, Pardner," the bartender asked in a subdued voice.

"Tombstone, Arizona," he replied.

"Sure must be tough over there," said the bartender.

"Yeah. In a way. They made me leave town."

"What! You? How could they make a man such as you get out?"

"Ah! They only let tough hombres stay. They claimed I was a sissy!"

———————

He woke up with such a headache as wouldn't fit into a hayloft.

———————

This Englisman's appraisal of an American farmer was printed in 1830. Doubtless they value us higher today. One hopes!

"An American farmer brought a cart full of pigeons to Philadelphia market on a day there happened to be a glut of them, and could find no purchasers. Not caring to lug his load back home again, he offered to give them away. But the people, supposing they must be stolen, would not have them. He then drove his cart on and dropped three or four every ten yards, but somebody always picked them up, bawled, 'Mister, you are losing your pigeons' and threw them back into his cart. Mortified, the man stopped his horse, and leaned back, pretending to be asleep. Instantly, men, women and children set to work and stole every one of his pigeons.

———————

Once he got to the saloon, he begun to make calluses on his elbows by freightin' hisself with scamper juice, an' paintin' his tonsils. Man! Thet o'l boy was a walkin' whiskey vat!

Then there was the Arkansas newspaper editor who lacked material for his paper. So he printed the Ten Commandments.

Later, he got a letter: "Cancel my subscription. What I do is none of your damned business!"

———————

Them folks made me feel welcome as Santa Claus in an orphan asylum. I guess that's why they got more friends than there are fiddlers in hell.

———————

Just how does a man go about the business describing a cow—not what she looks like but what she truly is as one of God's creatures. Here is one attempt to do the description.

"The cow is a female quadruped with an alto voice and a countenance in which there is no guile. She collaborates with the pump in the production of a liquid called milk, provides the filler for hash, and at last is skinned by those she has benefited, as mortals commonly are. The young cow is called a calf, and is used in the manufacture of chicken salad.

The cow's tail is mounted aft and has a universal joint. It is used to disturb marauding flies, and the tassel on the end has unique educational value. Persons who milk cows and come often in contact with the tassel have vocabularies of peculiar and impressive force.

The cow has two stomachs. The one on the ground floor is used as a warehouse and has no other function. When this one is filled, the cow retires to a quiet place, where her ill manners will occasion no comment, and devotes herself to belching. The raw material thus conveyed for the second time to the interior of her face is pulverized and delivered to the auxiliary stomach, where it is converted into cow.

The cow has no upper plate. All of her teeth are parked in the lower part of her face. As a results, she bites up and gums down.

A slice of cow is worth 65¢ in the cow, $2.50 in the hands of packers, and $12.50 in a restaurant that specializes in atmosphere."

That gent was dressed up fancy as the king of spades.

Then there was the Congressman from the farm district who was shrewd enough but a bit short on "book larnin." He needed his gun to go goose shooting and called his secretary to send the gun to him.

"I can't quite catch that word," she told him. "Such a bad connection. Please spell it."

"G as in Jesus, U as in onion, N as in pneumonia—GUN! Ya got it now?"

His eyes was blind as a posthole and twict as round.

Down in Oklahoma, a poultryman tried to save money by mixing ever increasing quantities of sawdust in the feed. But he had to quit the mix because his hens laid knotholes that hatched out chicks with wooden legs.

Wow! That whiskey is strong enough to make a jackrabbit spit in a bobcat's eye.

A Texas cowman at a convention for farmers and ranchers fell into a conversation with a New England farmer. Of course, the cowman bragged about the heroes of the Alamo—Crockett, Bowie and the other great men. Finally, the New Englander interrutped him, saying, "Those fellows don't hold a candle to our Paul Revere. . . ."

"Oh yeah, him," said the Texan. "Wasn't he the feller who rode hossback all one night hollerin' fer help?"

If you gargled that brand of hooch you was sure to annex a few queer animals.

We didn't drink too much. We was just over-served, is all.

A farmer came to town once a week, each time visiting the local store to buy hoe-handles, ten each visit. After a few weeks, the storekeeper asked him what he did with all of the hoe handles.

"I sell 'em to my neighbors," he said. "Get five bucks apiece for 'em!"

"Five bucks!" exclaimed the storekeeper. "But man! They cost you $7.00 each. You lose $2.00 on every one you sell."

"Yep. Sure do, but it beats farmin'."

That feller wasn't real drunk. No, he had took on what ya might call "a talkin' load."

Two ranchers, a bit "deef," sat at the bar, slowly sipping their whiskey.

"Windy, ain't it!" one old boy remarked.

"Nope. 'Tain't. It's Thursday."

"Yeah? Well so am I. Let's have us another drink."

He never knew he had a twin brother till he looked in the mirror hangin' back of the bar.

A Minnesota farmer made his first trip to Chicago. At this hotel he discovered the rooms were named after the states of the Union. The Texas room was big as a mansion. The Rhode Island room that he occupied was so small, so small, he said, that the furniture was painted on the wall. They gave him a crutch to keep him in bed, and he had to go out in the hall to turn around or to change his mind. And he had to teach his dog to wag his tail up and down for lack of space to wag sideways.

The names given whiskey during the time the west was being

won, are innovative and descriptive. Here are a few: coffin varnish, base-burner, conversation fluid, gut-warmer, neck-oil, red disturbance, redeye, scamper juice, snake poison, tonsil varnish, tornado juice, wild mare's milk. . . .

A city boy thought it would be fun to work on a farm. He was hired and given the job of cutting down hedge trees and sawing them into 7' lengths for fence posts. At the end of the day, the farmer drove out to see how the young man had done. There were only six posts out. "Here! Let me show you how" the irritated farmer said. "I thought you said you know how to saw logs."

"I do, I do," the city boy cried.

The farmer pulled the cord to start the saw and it went "BZ-BZ-BZZZZZ."

"What's that noise!" cried the startled lad.

With permission of *Country Magazine*

He took to his new job like a bear possum to a honey tree.

Then there was the Arizona cotton farmer who loved to experiment. He planted 33⅓% cotton, 33⅓% dacron and 33⅓% orlon. He plans to crossbreed the three varieties, then inbreed the progeny so as to get a single fibre incorporating the virtues of each variety. This fibre can be spun into a yarn that can be woven into a fabric having all the superior qualities of cotton with those of the synthetics. Now if that doesn't illustrate American genius and adaptability, we don't know what does.

"Yes, they do look a little like me."

With permission of *Country Magazine*

Gals back then didn't show near as much fetlock.

Speaking of ingenius breeders, how about the Oklahoma rancher who decided to raise kangaroos, then cross them with minks so that the result would be fur coats with pockets.

Both Texas and California grow large, tasty fruit. And each is jealous of the other. One day, a Texan and a Californian were looking at a lovely watermelon from the latter state. "My, but isn't that a gorgeous fruit," the Californian bragged.

"That puny anemic thing? Why, we'd hardly dignify it in Texas by admitting it's a watermelon."

"Watermelon!" exclaimed the Californian. "Man, you're blind. That's a California grape!"

Colder than a former sweetheart's kiss.

An old timer married a much younger woman and the union wasn't going well. The elderly farmer visited a marriage counselor who advised more affection. "Kiss and hug her oftener, several times a day. Show more affection," the counselor advised.

"How can I do that when I'm out in the field cultivating my crop? Takes me too long to get back to the house."

"So take a shotgun on the tractor and fire it when you feel romantic. She's young. She'll come running out to you."

A few weeks later the marriage counselor saw the farmer walking down the street. He asked: "How'd my plan work for you?"

"Went real good for a week or so," groaned the farmer, "then hunting season opened and I ain't seen her since."

How fat was she? Well, I'd say she was wide as two axe handles and a chaw of tobaccee.

A city man owned a large farm to which he sent his son to get farming experience. Having been raised on a farm, the man knew how valuable a farm background could be.

After one month, he phoned the farmer who operated his farm and asked how his son was performing.

The tenant farmer replied, "I've got to be honest with you—even if you are my landlord. But if that boy of yours had just one more hand, he'd need a third pocket to keep it in!"

That hired hand was about as lively as a thirty-year-old stud.

The Vermont farmer was visiting New York City for the first time. His nephew, Tom, who worked in the city, accompanied him as they walked down 7th Avenue. "It's a right nice town you got here, Tom, but hit looks to me like the folks here is mighty far behind in their haulin'."

That feller was so narrow-minded he could peek through a keyhole with both eyes at the same time.

A Mississippi farmer met a friend in town. Asked how things were on his farm, the old boy replied:

"Ain't no good, George. Las yeah the boll weavil, he et up most of mah cotton. Now Ah got a dang good crop but they don't pay nothin' fer it. All Ah can say is . . . if thangs don't git bettuh real soon Ah'll go to preachin' the gospel. Ah've done it before and Ah ain't a bit too good to do it agin."

Thet ol' cotton farmer was plumb talkative. Suffered from diarrhea of the jawbone.

Down in Georgia, a traveler bogged down in the adhesive-like clay. He had to pay a farmer $20.00 to pull him out. "Seems to me that you'd be so busy pulling folks out of these lousy mud roads that you'd be doing it day and night."

"Nope. Cain't pull em' out at night," drawled the farmer. "Night's when we'uns tote water to muddy the road!"

He was some unwelcome around here, about as welcome as a polecat at a picnic or a wet dog at an old maid's party. Anyhow, the folks here went around him like a swamp.

Two old farmers were reminiscing while sitting around the stove at the town store. "Ain't nobody ever licked me but once," one old boy remarked. "When I was a boy of ten years or so, I made the mistake of tellin' the truth and it cost me a beatin'."

"Might of cost you a beatin', but it sure cured ya."

His house was so small he couldn't cuss out his cat without gittin' fur in his mouth.

A farmer, quite able at his work but inexperienced in business, spent half a day with his mule, trying to pull a city man's car out of the bottomless mud near his farmstead. When he got back to the house two hours late for dinner, his wife said, "I sure hope you charged him good for all that work and half day lost!"

"Three dollars."

"Three dollars!" she screamed. "For all that work, I swear to goodness, George, but you'd have done better if you pulled the car out of the mud and let your mule handle the executive end of our business."

His brain size wouldn't make a drinkin' cup for a bumble bee.

What he really said was as unexpected and surprising as gunplay and cusswords in a Bible class. When it comes to cussin', he don't swallow his tongue none, but lets out a string that'd sizzle bacon. He was havin' a big old time airin' his lungs. To tell the truth, his language would make a bull-whacker hide his head in shame. He just took off the lid to the can of cusswords, and let 'em loose.

The youngster was late for school. Teacher was furious. "Tommy, you're late again. Now what's your excuse?"

"Well, Ma'am, I had to take the cow. . . ."

"Couldn't your Pa or the hired man have done it?" she interrupted the boy.

"Heck no, Ma'am, Pa or Pete ain't registered."

Skinny! Why that kid is so thin if he closed one eye he'd look like a needle. And he was so poorly his shadow was developin' holes and lookin' frazzled. He had to stand in one place twice to cast a shadow. Why, he's so thin he had to lean against a post to cuss. And do you know that last Saturday night he took a bath in his Pa's shotgun barrel! His young hide flaps on his bones jest like a bedquilt does on a backyard ridge pole.

———————

The farmer was anxious to have his son finish school so that he could begin a career on the farm. But when he approached the University to evaluate the courses, he protested that his son hadn't enough time for all those courses. Wasn't there a way to do it quicker, he asked.

"Yes, there is," responded the curriculum advisor, "it all depends on what you want to make of him. When God makes an oak tree, it takes Him a hundred years to do the job. But He needs only a couple of months to make a squash."

———————

He's a square shooter. You can ride the river with him 'cause he's got a heart straight as a rifle barrel. And he's honest as a looking glass. What's more, his word is as binding as a hangman's knot.

———————

The much-maligned traveling salesman came to the farmhouse very late at night. He begged for shelter and was told: "We're kinda crowded here, but you can take your choice. Sleep with baby or in the machine shed." The salesman didn' care to sleep with a baby, so he retired in the machine shed.

The next morning, walking to the house, he met a very pretty girl. "Who are you?"

"They call me Baby. Who are you?"

"I'm the damned fool that slept in the machine shed."

———————

He liked dancin' as well as cheatin' at cards. So they took him out and let him do a mid-air ballet from a cottonwood.

An elderly farmer saw an ad for a hearing aid for $39.95. A bargain! He rushed to the town and to the audiologist who was such a good salesman that the old farmer walked out with the best hearing aid in the house—$1500.

Walking down the street he met a neighbor. "George! How are you?" the neighbor asked. "Fine, thanks, just fine. Got a new hearing aid and it's great! Feller sold it to me was some salesman. Went in for one advertised for $39.95 and that derned salesman sold me this one for $1500!"

"Yeah! Fifteen hundred dollars! What kind is it?"

"It's a quarter past two!"

That feller was worthless. And untrustworthy. Why, if you was to sleep next to him, you'd best keep yore mouth shut if ya had gold teeth. I wouldn't trust that rascal far as I can throw an elephant against the wind. You shore are at risk if ya do business with him cause he ain't worth shucks.

During the terrible drought of 1988, the Irish Grove Presbyterian Church held services to pray for rain. It was a most earnest session. The preacher prayed: "Dear Lord, we gather here to ask for rain to save our corn and soybeans, our hay and oats, our gardens and trees. We got to have it, Lord, and the Good Book says if we have faith, pray with faith, we get answered. Without faith, we don't. Unfortunately, as I look over this congregation, I doubt if the necessary faith is there.

"How do I know? Just look around you, brothers and sisters, not a single one of you had the faith to bring an umbrella or a raincoat!"

And the Sheriff in Pyote County, Texas, is really tough. "How tough is he?" asked a rancher from Oklahoma.

"He's so tough he wears his silver star pinned to his chest."

"Shucks!" That doesn't sound so tough. Our sheriff back home does the same."

"Yes, but here he does it without a shirt!"

He'd fight a rattler and give him first strike.

American Cat Limited Partnership— 1980 A
AMOUNT: $1,250,000.00

PURPOSE: To establish cat skinning ranch at Pyote, Texas.

ANTICIPATED TAX SHELTER: First Year – $1,075,000.00
2nd Year – Who Knows
3rd Year – Infinity

FINANCIAL STRUCTURE: Equity – 100%

METHOD OF OPERATION: Buy cat ranch near Pyote, Texas
Buy 1 million cats
Buy 1 million rats

Each cat averages about twelve kittens a year; skins can be sold for about 20¢ for the white ones and up to 40¢ for a prime jet black pelt. This will give us 12 million cat skins per year to sell at an average of around 32, making our revenue about $3,000,000 a year. This really averages out to $10,000 a day—excluding Sundays and holidays.

A good Texan cat man can skin about 50 cats per day at a rate of $3.15 a day. It will only take 663 men to operate the ranch so the net profit will be over $8,200 per day.

Now the cats will be fed on rats exclusively. Rats multiply four times as fast as cats. We will start a rat ranch right adjacent to our cat farm. Here is where the first year tax break really comes in. Since we will be utilizing the rats to beed the cats, we can expense the entire first batch of rats purchased during 1980. If we start with one million rats, at a nickel each, we will have four rats per cat per day, and a whopping $50,000 1980 tax deduction.

The rats will feed on the carcasses of the cats we skin during 1981 and successive years. This will give each rat one-quarter of a cat. You can see by this that the business is a clean operation, self-supporting, and really automatic throughout. The cats will eat the rats and the rats will eat the cats, and we will get the skins and the tax benefits; incidentally, the ecologists think it's great.

Eventually, we hope to cross the cats with snakes. Snakes skin themselves twice a year. This will save the labor costs of skinning and will also give us a yield of two skins for one cat.

Let me know as soon as possible if you are interested. Naturally, we want to keep this excellent deal limited to the fewest investors possible. Time is of the essence!

Sincerely,

I.M. Line

A rancher's wife called the newspaper to ask the cost of a funeral announcement. "We charge three dollars an inch, ma'am," the clerk replied.

"Holy smokes!" the wife exclaimed. "That's gonna cost me a fortune. My John was six feet six!"

A farmer asked his physician how the lawyer, of whom they were both clients, was feeling.

"He's lying at death's door."

"He always had courage, all right. Imagine! Him at death's door and still lyin'."

No use kickin' . . . unless you're a mule.

Driving along a country road, a man noticed a chicken running beside the car. He speeded up. The chicken stayed even. Forty, then fifty, then sixty miles an hour and still that chicken ran alongside.

The man slowed to a stop, then, curious, he followed the chicken back down the road, noticing the bird had three legs. When the three-legged chicken turned in at a farmhouse, the man stopped the car and went to the door. The farmer opened it. "Say, I'm sure curious about that three-legged chicken," he announced.

"Lots of folks are. Y'see, my family loves drumsticks. So I bred a chicken with three legs."

"Great idea," said the visitor.

"How do they taste?"

"Don't know. Haven't yet caught one!"

"For some reason I have a feeling
the garden isn't going to come up."

With permission of *Country Magazine*

He moved quicker'n an old maid can crawl under a bed.

The grass was so pore the cows looked like the runnin' gear of a grasshopper.

The farm wife instructed the hired man just where to plant her seedling "Salivas."

"But ma'am, that's pronounced 'Salvia' and not 'Saliva'," the hired man explained.

"Just do it and don't tell me how to pronouce Salivas," she told him. "Then when you get them Salivas finished, put a ring of Petunias around them."

"Yes, ma'am," the hired man said, "but, Mrs., I kinda think it'd be a whole lot safer to plant Spitoonia to support and hold that Saliva of yours."

Some folks can't see a joke except by appointment and most of them would be late, at that.

A farmer returned from his annual visit to his physician.
"How are you dear? Everything all right?" his wife asked.
"Yes. Nothing that a daily dose of acetyl . . . acetycalic . . . calic . . . won't keep under control."
"Oh! You mean aspirin?"
"Dang! I never can remember that name."

That old boy didn't have a nickel to his name. But he'd go out to the pond, throw in his line, lean back against a tree, grin and say, "I wonder what the poor people are doin' today."

The newest public health discovery: never lend money. It gives people amnesia!

He's one of them guys that'd lend ya an umbrella when the sun was shinin' but take it back soon as a rain come up.

The stern banker reviewed the farmer's loan application while the farmer nervously fidgited in his chair. At last the banker nodded. "All seems to be in order and satisfactory with your assets. Now, sir, could you tell me about your liabilities?"
"No problem. Ain't nobody able to lie better'n me."

His luck raveled out, cleanin' him 'till he was nekkid down to his spurs.

The lady returned her rented horse to the stable. "That's a mighty polite horse you folks rented me," she told the attendant.

"What do you mean?"

"Well, we came to a fence and he let me go over first."

How sad the story of Jane McCleek,
Her will was strong, but her won't was weak.

The township sage remarked that it would be a better world if we loved our neighbors as we love ourselves. But, he went on, it's a question if they could stand all that affection!

Farmers have got to quit looking to Washington for leadership. It's hopeless. The great man died in 1799!

It's clear that the reason why there were fewer farm accidents in horse-and wagon days was that the driver did not have to rely solely on his own intelligence.

I went to the men's room and, come time fer it, I picked up a towel that was plumb popular judgin' by it's complexion.

At a famous Texan's funeral, one of the mourners remarked that it was a tiny casket and seemed much too small for a man as big as the deceased.

"No! It fits him perfectly," a bystander remarked, "after they let all the bullshit out of him."

Suits me fine. Like a dead hoss . . . I ain't kickin'.

They tell the story in Texas of one of their rich oil men who had dinner at a fashionable restaurant. When he had finished, he deposited a $100 bill for the tip!

The waiter ran after him exclaiming that he'd made a mistake or forgotten to pick up the large sum.

"It ain't no mistake, boy, and jist you remember it. Next time I come you better give a whole lot better service!"

He was jumpy as popcorn on a hot skillet.

A hog and a hen were having a discussion about responsibility. The hog explained it as follows. "Consider it like a breakfast of ham and eggs. For you it's only a donation. But for me it's a total commitment."

That little ol' baby made more noise than a wagon load of tin pans on a frozen pond.

A farmer was feeling poorly. He visited his doctor who gave him a fistful of prescriptions that he took to his pharmacist.

"Tell me sir," the pharmacist asked, "how do you want to arrange financing?"

"Let's see now . . . corn up three . . . beans down two . . ."

With permission of *Country Magazine*

The Strange New Water Closet

Right after the turn of the century a man was heard speaking down at the local barber shop in Kansas City. He was normally a reserved man, yielding the floor to the more aggressive and loud yarn-spinners, but today he was wound up. He was excited. And his audience was all ears listening to him tell his story:

"My wife sent off to Monkey Wards for one of them newfangled things called a water closet. Or was it Sears and R'ar Back? Anyhow, the whole kit-and-kaboottle is called a bathroom, and let me tell you boys, is it ever fancy!

"Now, it has to be in-stalled by a man called a plummer. On one side of the room is a big long thing that looks like a hog-trough, except it's smooth, and that's where you get in and waller around and wash yourself all over. On the other side of the room is a little white thing called a sink, with a stopper in the bottom. This is where you take your 'possible baths.' You know, you wash up as far as possible, or you wash down as far as possible, and if nobody's looking, why, you hit ole possible a lick or two.

"But, now, I'll tell you what takes the cake. The footwasher! Fellers, it sits over in the corner and you ain't never seen a contraption like it. Why, you put in one foot and wash it, then pull this chain, and, swoosh! you've got clean water for the other foot.

"Two lids came with that foot-washer, and I'm danged if we can figure out what they're for. So we're using one for a bread board, and the other one, the one that had a big hole in it, we used that one to frame Grandpa's picture with. And I'll tell you something, now, that company is on the ball. They're fine folks to do business with. They sent us a whole roll of writing paper with it, free of charge!"

*Reprinted with permission from: "Outhouse Humor"
Billy Edd Wheeler. August House
Little Rock, AR 1988

Nope, I ain't him. I reckon you done smelt out the wrong hound's butt, mister.

Texas is known for tall talk. The British aren't far behind. Once a British sailor was telling a Texas cowboy that the ship he was on was so big the captain had to go around the deck in a jeep.

The Texas pooh-poohed the British Navy. "Why," he declaimed, "the kitchen in our flagship is so humongous that the cook has to go through the Irish stew in a submarine to see if the potatoes are done."

There ain't much paw and beller to a man as gits things done.

A cowboy was telling about the death of his boss, a man notoriously hard on his men.

"What was the complaint?" a listener asked.

"Ain't no complaint. Everybody wuz satisfied!"

He reached for his gun but before he could tetch it he was on his way to St. Peter to take harp lessons.

The overweight farmer explained how effective the "fat farm" had been in allowing him to lose weight. "Why, I spent three days there and I was $750 lighter!"

He wasn't too fat. Not overweight one bit. It was just that they made him a foot too short.

He was born full growed and began gettin' big from there on.

Then old Packsaddle Jack got to telling about Senator Dorsey, of Star Route fame, selling a little herd of cattle he had in northern New Mexico. He said the Senator had got hold of some eye-glass Englighmen, and, representing to them that he had a large herd of cattle, finally made a sale at $25 a head all around. The Englishmen however, insisted on counting the herd and wouldn't take the Senator's books for them. Dorsey agreed to this; he then went to his foreman, Jack Hill.

"Jack," he said, "I want you to find me a small mountain around which a herd of cattle can be circled several times in one day. This mountain must have a kind of natural stand where men can get a good count on cattle stringing by but where they can't possibly get a view of what is going on outside, Sabe?"

Jack selected a little round mountain with a canyon on one side of it. Here on the bank of the canyon he stationed the Englishmen and their bookkeepers and Senator Dorsey. The Senator had only about 1,000 cattle, and these Jack and the cowboys separated into two bunches out in the hills. Keeping the two herds about a mile apart, they now drove the first herd into the canyon . . . It was hardly out of sight before the second bunch came stringing along. Meantime cowboys galloped the first herd around back to the mountain and had them coming down the canyon past the Englishmen again for a second count. And they were hardly out of sight before the second division was around the mountain and coming along to be tallied again. Thus the good work went on all morning, the Senator and the Englishmen having only a few minutes to snatch a bite and tap fresh bottles.

At noon Dorsey's foreman told the English party that his men were yet holding an enormous herd back in the hills from which they were cutting off these small bunches of 500 and bringing them along to be tallied. But about three o'clock in the afternoon the cattle began to get thirsty and footsore. Every critter had already traveled thirty miles that day, and lots of them began to drop out and lie down. In one of the herds was an old yellow steer. He was bobtailed, lophorned, and had a game leg. When for the fifteenth time he limped by the crowd that was counting, milord screwed his eyeglass a little tighter on his eye and says:

"There is more bloody, blarsted, lophorned, bobtailed, yellow crippled brutes than anything else, it seems."

Milord's dogrobber speaks up and says, "But, me lord, there's no hanimal like 'im hin the other 'erd."

The Senator overheard this interesting conversation, and, taking the foreman aside, told him when they got that herd on the other side of the mountain again to cut out the old yellow reprobate and not let him come by again. So Jack cut him out and ran him off a ways. But old yellow had got trained to going around that mountain, and the herd wasn't any more than tallied again till here come old Buck, as the cowboys called him, limping down the canyon, the Englishmen staring at him with open mouths and Senator Dorsey looking at old Jack Hill in a reproachful, grieved kind of way. The cowboys ran old Buck off still farther next time, but half an hour afterwards he appeared over a little rise and slowly limped by again.

The Senator now announced that there was only one herd more to count and signalled to Jack to ride around and stop the cowboys. . . . But as the party broke up and started for the ranch, old Buck came by again, looking like he was in a trance. That night the cowboys said the Senator was groaning in his sleep in a frightful way, and when one of them woke him up and asked if he was sick, he told them, while big drops of cold sweat dropped off his face, that he'd had a terrible nightmare. He said that he thought he was yoked up with a yellow, bobtailed, lophorned, lame steer and was being dragged by the animal through a canyon and around a mountain, day after day, in a hot, broiling sun, while crowds of witless Englishmen and jibbering cowboys were looking on. He insisted on saddling up and going back through the moonlight to the mountain to see if old Buck was still there. A cowboy went with him and after they had got to the canyon and waited a while they heard something coming. Sure enough, directly in the bright moonlight they saw old Buck painfully limping along, stopping now and then to rest.

A week later a cowboy reported finding old Buck dead on his well-worn trail. No one ever rides that way on moonlight nights now, for the cowboys have a tradition that during each full moon old Buck's ghost still limps down the canyon.

*From COWBOY LIFE ON THE SIDETRACK. Frank E. Benton
Lincoln-Herndon Press, Inc.
818 S. Dirksen Parkway
Springfield, IL 1988.

Once upon a time there was a bovine family of papa cow,

mama cow and a little baby boy cow. They were happy until little boy cow turned up missing. His parents looked high and low for him day and night but had no luck. Alas! Then one day, at the top of a precipice, they saw him grazing in the valley far, far away. They were tickled pink! Then Mama cow turned to Papa cow and said: "That goes to show just how far a little bull will go!"

He stood out like a new saloon near a Baptist church.

A farm lady phoned to the sheriff that on Saturday night, a thief broke into her house and stole her bathtub. She said that whoever stole it can keep it but she sure would like to get back her Aunt Minerva.

You ain't got no more chance than a rabbit in a hound's mouth.

Everybody knows Pecos Bill, the Paul Bunyan of the Southwest. And old Pecos Bill's wife, Sluefoot Sue whom he cherished above all humans. That's why he forbid her to ride his one-man horse, Widow Maker. But, like a woman, Sluefoot Sue disobeyed orders (remember Eve and Adam?) and mounted Widow Maker who promptly tossed her up to the moon. When she came down she landed on her bustle and up she went. Then down. Then up. Finally, Pecos Bill found her abouncin' but couldn't hold her, nor lasso her, nor save her. To keep her from starving to death, he had to shoot her!

And Pecos Bill was the gentlest of souls. He never killed a woman (except Sluefoot Sue), a child or man (not even a tourist—except out of season!).

He was a real man, the one who put the spikes on cactus and the horns on toads. In his spare time he dug the Rio Grande when he got tired of hauling water from the Gulf of Mexico. And he laid-out New Mexico and used Arizona for his west pasture.

You may wonder what he died of. Well, ordinary whiskey had no kick for him so he laced his liqour with barbed wire and, likely, that's what killed him—not the barbs but the rust.

Any yet . . . and yet some say he died of a different cause . . . when he caught sight of a mid-western dude rigged up in a mail order cowboy outfit, they say he laughed himself to death.

Tough? That old Pecos Bill was the toughest gent west of anywhere east.

"What happened to that eastern gent who was visiting your ranch?" a friend at the bar asked the cowboys assembled there.

"Well, it was mighty sad. Yep. Shore war. The very fust mornin' this nice gent was abrushin' his teeth and old Packsaddle Jack, here, seen him a-foamin' at the mouth, figured he had the hydrophobia and shot him dead. Shore was sad!"

It wasn't that they dislike him; Nope! They jest figgered his neck was too short so they figured to take him out and stretch it.

That ol' boy's family tree was a stump and he was the runt son of old man trouble. He was meaner'n a rattlesnake on a hot tin skillet an' probably had a reserve seat in hell.

The fund-raising committee of the church called on an old rancher and asked for a contribution.

"Can't give a penny. Not this year!"

"But you must. You owe the Lord more than you owe anybody!"

"Couldn't argue with that. But the Lord ain't pushin' me like my other creditors!"

It shore is the truth when they say the bigger the mouth the better it looks shut.

With permission of *Country Magazine*

About that idea of yours. It's got as much chance as a wax cat in hell.

It seems that a man's health was bad and the doctor ordered him to go to Colorado, out in the mountains, and do nothing but rest for several months—cut off from the world, not even a letter from home, nothing to disturb him at all, and build up.

Three months later, he was feeling fit and fine, so he sent a wire that he was coming home and, when he stepped off the train in his home town, old Uncle Zeke was there with the station wagon to meet him and take him to his home, several miles out in the country.

The old negro said, "Marse Will, I'se shore powerful glad to see you. You is lookin' fine."

"I'm glad to see you, too, Zeke. I've been away a long time and my health has improved wonderfully. How are things at home? What's the news?"

"Marse Will, dere ain't no news—no news a-tall."

"Why, after all this time, there must be some news."

"Well, now, suh, lemme see. Oh yes, I do believe dare is a little. Yoah huntin' dog is dead."

"My hunting dog is dead? My fine pointer dead and yet you say there's no news. How in the world did he die?"

"Well, suh, dey say he musta died on account ob eatin' buhn'd hoss meat."

"Burned horse meat? How could that be?"

"Well, when de stable buhn'd."

"What, my fine stable burned down and you call that no news!"

"Yas, suh, de stable done buhn'd an' dem ridin' hosses jes' seem lak dey couldn't git out an' dey buhn'd up an' dat pointa dog got to sniffin' roun' aftuh de fiah an' et some ub de buhn'd hoss meat an' den he died."

"Great heavens! My dog dead, my stable burned up, my horses all gone. How did the fire start?"

"Well, dey claims de sparks frum de house—"

"Sparks from the house? Don't tell me that my house is gone!"

"Yas, suh, de house hit buhn'd an' hit seem lak some o' de sparks flew ovah an' lit on de stable—"

"My beautiful house gone and you tell me there's no news. How did the house catch on fire?"

"Well, Cunn'l, it musta been frum de candles."

"Candles! Why we never use candles in my home."

"Dese wuz by de coffin."

"What!"

"Yas, suh youah aunt dun died—"

"My aunt passed away; that fine old lady. This is too much."

"Yas, suh, she done died and dey had some candles settin' roun' an' one ub dem caught de curtains on fiah and dey couldn't stop it and de house jes' buhn'd down, dat's all."

"No news! My poor aunt dead, my home burned down, my

favorite dog dead, my horses all lost, my stables destroyed. How in the world did my aunt come to die?"

"Well suh, after your wife ran away wid de sho-fuh, she jes' naturally grieved huhself to death!"

I don't know where to start lookin'. I've got about as much chance of findin' it as findin' a hoss thief in heaven.

A group of Texans were at the saloon discussing why each had come to the Lone Star state.

One had killed a man; another had held up a bank; bigamy was another's problem. "Boys, I came to Texas for something I didn't do."

The cowboys hooted in disbelief until the fellow raised his hand for quiet.

"It was like this. Back in Illinois, they raised $25,000 to build a church. I was chairman of the fund drive and I came to Texas for not building that church.

A Missouri farmer drove his battered pickup truck to the toll bridge spanning the Mississippi River. "One dollar," said the toll keeper.

"Sold," said the farmer.

Cautious! Why, my boss is so cautious he'd ride a mile to spit.

An old couple, married fifty years, had never paid much attention to the refinements of life. They were too busy just living. But the wife had lately become interested in the customs and manners of polite society so that, one morning at breakfast, she said to her ancient husband: "Hiram, if you don't quit saucerin' and blowin' and drinkin' yore coffee out'n yore saucer I'm jist gonna up and leave ya."

The old boy looked up, considering the implications. Then he said: "Honey, I'm gonna miss ya."

He served us coffee made out of water thick enough to plow.

The farm boy ran to the nearest farmhouse and shouted at the farmer working in the home garden. "Come help my pa."

"What happened," said the farmer and ran toward the boy.

"He fell off the haywagon into the mud."

"Is he in very deep?"

"Yep. He's plumb up to his ankles."

"Aw, then he's not so bad off."

"Heck he ain't. He fell in head first."

When I got throwed, I hit so hard I liked to of took root and sprouted.

The members had decided to renovate and beautify their church cemetary by building an ornamental fence around it. But when it came time to raise funds to do the job, money was not easily obtained. One of the members voiced the sentiments of the majority when he said: "We ain't got no need atall for a fence around our cemetary. Those folks on the outside sure don't want to get in and them as is on the inside can't get out."

The Farm Bureau advisor was asked how long cows should be milked. He replied: "The same as short ones."

He was the tallest feller around, so tall he couldn't tell when his feet got cold. Why, he was long as a wagon track and built plenty high above his corns. Yep! It would take a steeple-jack to look him in the eye. His adam's apple had a six-inch plunge.

Shortly after the death of Pecos Bill, a young man, a neighbor of his got married and moved to a new ranch. After several weeks he was seen in town looking very sad.

"What's wrong, Jake?" he was asked.

"Lost my wife," he replied.

"How come."

"She fell an' broke her leg. Wasn't nothin' I could do but shoot her to save her from the miseries."

The trouble was, when he was about ten, somebody stole his rudder and he ain't been able to figure where he's at since.

A young man raised in seclusion in a distant area of the Adirondakes, took his first train ride. The hostess came around with snacks and the lad chose a banana. When the hostess returned and asked if he wanted another, the lad replied, "Nope. They're plumb tasty but they's jist too much cob."

He don't know manure from molasses.

They tell the story of the terrible drought of the thirties in Kansas. It seems that during that awful time, a heavy windstorm swept a barrel away from a settler's soddy and blew it for miles and miles. Then the wind reversed and blew the barrel back to the very cabin it had come from. However, the friction of the sand and rocks coupled with the force of the abrasive wind resulted in a returned barrel no bigger than a small keg.

Another similar story involves the same time in the same area with yet another barrel that, when returned, was no more than a mere *bunghole*. So the settler took that bunghole down to the coopersmith and that worthy built an entire new barrel around it. They were innovative in those days.

Somewhere along the way the heat must have crazied his think box.

PROGRESS!

FITS ALL SIZES!!

THAT BIG ONE IS FOR POLITICIANS

A traveler from the city was lost. He drove over back country roads for hours and seemed no closer to his destination. He stopped to question a youth sitting by the road. "How far is it to Tucson?"

"Dunno."

"Well then, am I headed in the right direction?"

"Dunno."

"Then you can perhaps tell me if I'm headed on the right road?"

"Dunno."

Out of patience, the traveler said, "You don't know much, do you?"

"Mebbe not. But I ain't lost."

"I KNOW each farmer feeds 55 other people,
but you can't list THAT many dependents!"

With permission of *Country Magazine*

Farmin's all he ever done. He's been a farmer since he shed his three-cornered pants.

By the way of entertainment, visitors to the historic village used to offer Flancy, the village idiot, a penny or a dime. And Flancy always chose the penny, the larger coin. So one day a visitor asked him why he took the penny instead of the dime. "Because ef I ever took the dime, you can bet yore boots those dern fools would quit offerin' money to me."

It shore was peaceful out there, 'bout like a thumb in a baby's mouth.

An Arizona farmer left an unusual request with the funeral director when he made arrangments for his interment.
"I want to be buried together with my trusty old pick-up truck." The undertaker tried to talk him out of the bizarre request. "Nope. You're gonna do it or I'll go someplace else." Asked why, he replied, "I'll tell ya why. I ain't never seen a hole that dern jalopy couldn't git me out of."

The real estate agent swung his arm toward the vast area of sandy, treeless and desolate dust bowl country. "It's a wonderful place. All we need is good people and water." "Yeah," said the traveler. "And that's all hell needs."

Ever' time thet ol' boy gits into trouble, he gits out of it by gittin' down on his prayer-bones and taffyin' the Lord up.

A Montana rancher counseled a newcomer to the area. "We got trouble out here so high that you cain't climb it, so wide ya cain't git around it and so dang deep that ya cain't dig out of it. So . . . the only way to whip it is to jest duck yore head, grit yore teeth and wade right on through it!"

You can depend on him till they cut ice in Death Valley.

A Nebraska farmer wrote his last will and testament as follows:

FITS ALL SIZES

HERE'S WHY

NO HOLES: SIMPLY TWO BOARDS ALL THE WAY ACROSS.

SPEAKING OF HOLES.... ROUND, OVAL, SQUARE, HEX, DIAMOND. TO MENTION ONLY A FEW.

THEN_ SOME HAD LIDS TO COVER 'EM UP.

MAYBE FUR LINING ON SOME ...

With permission of George Borum, Olney, IL

"To my wife, I leave my overdraft at the bank. She can explain it.

"The equity in my truck I leave to my son who will have to go to work to keep up the payments.

"To my landlord I leave the outbuildings he made me put up. He's the only one who ever made any money off the farm, anyway.

"Any to the junkman I leave my equipment because he's going to get it anyway.

"And last . . . I want six pallbearers all of them to be my creditors. They've carried me this far and they'd just as well finish the job."

He was some careful, all right, about like a preacher talking to the devil.

A cloudburst inundated the entire farm and flooded so deeply that the family had to go to the attic. The next morning, the father looked out the attic window and noticed a straw hat drifting back and forth over the south pasture. He watched it go slowly from one side to the other and exclaimed: "What in the world is that hat doing out there?"

"Oh, that's Uncle Elmer," one of the boys said. "He told us he was agonna mow that south pasture come hell or high water!"

It jest kept on rainin' like the Lord Hisself had pulled the cork. I got to wishin' I'd growed fins instead of feet. But we shore needed that rain and, when she started, I hope she'd keep on till I had to dive down so as to check the water tower.

In Calhoun County, Illinois they tell the story of the farmer who was proud of how broadminded he was. He had his hats specially made *oversized* so that everybody would know how truly broad-minded he was. It was this same *broad-minded* feller who said he didn't care to accumulate much land. All he wanted was the land that adjoined his.

———————

That feller is so tight he wouldn't lend ya a nickel less'n you got the Lord and a passel of angels to go on yore note.

———————

Two men were discussing the effect of marriage on a man. One fellow said he'd never known a married man who was the boss in his home. That set the other to wondering. They talked about it for a time and decided to run an actual test to see what was the true proportion of men who bossed their own homes.

So, they decided to load watermelons in the half-ton blue Chevy pickup truck owned by the one man and to give a melon to every household where the woman was boss. If the man was boss, they'd give him one of their trucks.

So they started off in the half-ton blue pickup and the one-ton white truck. Before half the day was over they'd given most of their melons away. Then they spotted a farmhouse where the man was sitting on the front porch while the wife was busy digging a ditch along the side of the house.

They stopped and told the man why they were there. "Fine," he said. "I'll take the one-ton white job."

Just then his wife came over and told him he'd made a bad choice.

"Mind your own business, woman, I know what truck I want."

"Yes, dear, I respect your wishes. But the truth is, we'd be a lot better off with the half-ton blue pickup." She called him aside and they chatted for a few minutes. Then the married man came over and said, "I've changed my mind, fellers. I've decided to take the half-ton blue pickup, afterall."

"Sorry buster," said the visitors. "Now all you get is watermelon."

The hardest that man ever worked was to take a quick squint at the sun and then hunker down in the shade.

For those who like watermelons but are sometimes disappointed in the melon they pick at the store . . . not ripe enough . . . here is an Ohio plan to make the selection of melons foolproof. When the melon is small, the grower inserts a small whistle. As it grows and ripens, gas forms and toots the whistle informing the grower that the melon is ready.

The inventor is planning to have whistles of various keys and tones so that a field will play harmonic music similar to a symphony, bringing people to the farm from miles around. Thus, the music will create a built-in audience of customers saving the cost of hauling melons to market . . . The inventor-farmer is looking for investors and readers who are interested may address their inquiry to the publisher who will forward the information to the genius inventor-farmer

---

That li'l gadget made more noise than an old sow with her tit caught under the gate.

Late at night, a motorist lost in the piney woods stopped at a farmhouse to ask for shelter. It was granted him. He retired early to awaken the next morning, quite refreshed. He was on the back porch brushing his teeth, combing his hair, lathering, shaving, lotioning and deodorizing himself for the day.

The young son of the farmer watched him go through all these morning ablutions. "Mister," the boy asked, "are you this much trouble to yourself every morning?"

He felt as much out of place as a camel in the Klondike.

The cowboys had been driving cattle for days and the last

two days they were without water. Then they came upon a stream. The cattle rushed in and all the cowboys but one went upstream to clean water. But one cowboy stayed behind the cattle and scooped up the muddy water and drank out of his hat. "Come on up here!" the cowboys called to him: "Hey, Shorty! Clean water up here."

"Hit don't matter, boys. I aim to drink it all anyways."

The water over there needs chawin' before ya can swailer it, but if yore thirsty, well, it makes damn good drinkin'.

The traveling salesman so famous in farm stories, ran out of gas on a lonely road, then walked to a farmhouse and asked if he could stay the night. "Sure. Come right on in," the farmer greeted him. "You're welcome. But you'll have to share a room with my son."

"Good golly," gasped the salesman. "I'm in the wrong joke."

Him? Smart? Hell, he don't know sic'em!

It was so hot and dry the bushes were followin' the dogs around.

The farmer was a chronic complainer. For years, he complained, the weather had been against him, the bugs had eaten up what little produce he could grow, and always the market was low when something was ready to sell. Then came the year when he hit it big. No bugs, perfect weather, a huge crop and high prices.

"Well, you finally made it big," a friend said.

"Fair, just fair," the farmer said. "Just think what a big crop like this takes out of the soil!"

I got so hot buckin' bales that if somebody had stuck a fork in me they'd have found me well done.

A college freshman applied for a farm job during his summer vocation. He was a track star but had never done any farm work. But he was willing and eager so that when the farmer sent him out to round up the sheep and bring them in off pasture for the night, the young man trotted off eagerly.

The lad was gone a long time. At last, hot and sweaty, he came jogging over the hill to the farmhouse and announced that all the sheep and lambs were safely in the corral. "But I don't have any lambs," the farmer replied.

"You sure as heck do. I had a heluva time getting them to come in with their parents. But I made it," he said, triumphantly.

The farmer hurried to the corral to investigate. There he found a dozen jackrabbits along with the exhausted sheep!

"He said his first dirty word—'vegetarian'. . . !"

That city dude couldn't ride nothin' wilder'n a wheel chair.

Her face looked like the east end of a jackass going west.

Then there was this older rancher who got married to a young and beautiful wife and he just simply couldn't keep his hands off her. Finally, he had to fire every one of them.

That ol' boy is loaded to the muzzle with mad. He's mad enough to swaller the devil, horns and all.

A lanky Kentucky farmer came to the village store and with him were his young, pretty wife and her week-old baby.

They were greeted by the storekeeper who said: "Mighty glad to see you young folks. Is that yore young 'un, Lem?"

The young father thought a few minutes, then replied: "I reckon so. Leastwise, it was caught in my trap."

He is slow actin' as wet gunpowder.

With the proliferation and frequent sales at country auctions, old Mrs. Beebe decided to visit one to see what went on at these affairs. She came in just as the bidding grew hottest for a very rare, hand-blown whisky bottle. She walked close to where the bottle stood on a pedestal looked it over and gasped: "Gawdamighty! It's *empty!*"

A traveler stopped at a store in a small country town in Kansas when it was devastated with a year-long drought. He inquired of the proprietor behind the counter, "Can you please tell me where we can find a camping place under some trees and near water?"

The owner eyed the tourist a moment, then spoke softly, "Well, God bless you for the thought, mister."

The preacher was visiting two of his richest, most respected parishioners, two quite elderly "unclaimed treasures" or, as folks say . . . "spinster ladies." Theirs was a lovely old brick mansion filled with exquisite antiques and the preacher enjoyed moving about the lovely front parlor to examine all the lovely artifacts in the elegant room.

As he passed the grand piano, he accidentally knocked a small cardboard box off it onto the floor. He picked up the box, looked at it and gasped: "Ladies! Dear ladies! I am speechless to find this box of ... of ... condoms in this virtuous, pious and absolutely faultless home. I ... just ... don't understand."

The one old maid, Pricilla, looked at her sister, Mayrose, and said: "Perhaps you'd better tell him about us and our discovery that has completely changed our outlook on life. Mayrose, you can explain it so much better than I. Oh, Parson Jones! That box had so enriched our lives."

Preacher Jones drew in his breath sharply, shaking his head in dismay and confusion.

Mayrose tittered, blushed, began: "Well, Parson Jones, when our beloved father passed to his eternal reward, it was required of us that we go through his effects. And we did. In his work desk we found this little box that has changed our life . . . right, Prissy?"

"Certainly right, Mayrose. Go on and tell him. It can help him and the entire parish."

Parson Jones was pale and shaking. With one arm, he reached for the arm of the chair behind him and sank into it, holding his head with his free hand.

"Well, Parson Jones, to continue . . . The instructions on that lovely boxed discovery you picked off the floor were to place it on the organ! To prevent disease! We didn't have an organ, only a piano, so we placed it where you found it and unfortunately, knocked it to the floor. It has remained on our organ ... er ... piano ever since. And, dear Parson Jones, do you know that neither Priscilla nor I have had a single disease since we placed it on our organ . . . I mean piano . . . over seven years ago!"

He hardly ever went to church. Y'see, most of his religion was in his wife's name. Listenin' to Psalms and hollerin' wasn't his plate of beans.

The oldest living farmer in his community had reached the noble age of eighty-five. The editor of the county weekly newspaper, came to review his life for a feature article. When the editor had completed his interview, he leaned back and began a social conversation. They chatted a bit and then the editor asked: "I suppose that when a man reaches your august age, his sex life is concluded and of the past?"

"Oh no! Not at all. Not at all. Except . . . except for the last two weeks when it has been kinda dead."

"Oh? Have you been sick?"

"No, not at all. I been feelin' good as a stud goat. But the feller who puts me on and then lifts me off . . . he's been sick."

He was so weak he had to lean against a post to spit. Why, he didn't have enough wind to blow out a candle. And when he coughed, man alive, he sounded like the overture to a funeral.

A tragedy occured in Kansas, recently, when a terrible twister carried off a farmer's house, furniture and four children. In country tradition, the neighbors pooled resources to give the bereaved, bereft farmer a fresh start. They donated a new bed for him and his wife.

She's buildin' a nest.

Under auspices of the Extension Service of the University of Illinois, a farmer who had constantly complained to them that farm wives, including his own, did not do their share of the hard farm work, suggested a study. The farmer was to do all the chores his wife did, every day, and keep a record of his every move. The published results of the study were as follows:

Lost temper: 52 times.

I got so hungry that my equator was plumb narrow.

"It's such a nice day we thought we'd eat out."

Josh Billings (Herny Wheeler Shaw) was the most popular humorist of the last century. Abraham Lincoln is said to have remarked: "Josh Billings is the best judge of human nature since Shakespeare." He has the dry, wise and witty humor of the New Englander and his observations on man, beast and vegetable are as wise and funny today as back then. His use of phonetic spelling (and why not spell words the way they sound?) may slow the reader a bit. But, in a few paragraphs, the reading is easy. And Josh Billings is always fun. He has been called "THE AMERICAN ECCLESIASTES."

ESSAY ON SWINE

Hogs generally are quadruped.

The extreme length ov their antiquity has never been fully discovered; they existed a long time before the flood, and have existed a long time since.

There iz a great deal ov internal revenue in a hog, there ain't much more waste in them than there iz in a oyster.

Even their tails can be worked up into whistles.

Hogs are good quiet boarders; they always eat what iz set

before them, and don't ask any foolish questions.

They never have any disease but the measles, and they never have that but once; once seems to satisfy them.

There iz a great many breeds amongst them.

Some are a close corporation breed, and some are bilt more apart, like a hemlock slab.

Sum are full in the face, like a town clock, and some are az long and lean az a cow-catcher, with a steel-pointed noze on them.

They can all root well; a hog that can't root well, haz bin made in vain.

They are a short-lived animal, and generally die az soon az they git fat.

The hog can be learnt a great many cunning things, such az heisting the front gate off from the hinges, tipping over the swill barrells, and finding a hole in the fence to git into a corn-field, but there ain't any length tew their memory; it iz awful hard work for them tew find the same hole to git out at, especially if you are at all anxious they should.

Hogs are very contrary, and seldom drive well the same way you are going; they drive the most the other way; this haz never bin fully explained, but speaks volumes for the hog.

———

He humps his back like a hog goin' to war.

———

THE MULE*

The mule is half hoss and half Jackass, and then comes tew a full stop, natur discovering her mistake.

They weigh more, accordin tu their heft, than any other creature, except a crowbar.

They can't hear any quicker, nor further than the hoss, yet their ears are big enough for snow shoes.

You can trust them with any one whose life ain't worth any more than the mules. The only way tew keep the mules into a

*This is the first published article that Josh was paid for ($1.50). It was published across the nation and brought him national publicity and he went on to national and international fame.

pasture is tew turn them into a meadow joining, and let them jump out.

They are ready for use, just as soon as they will do tew abuse.

They haint got any friends, and will live on huckle berry brush, with an occasional chance at Canada thistels.

They are a modern invention, i don't think the Bible deludes tew them at tall.

Tha sell for more money than any other domestic animile. You cant tell their age by looking into their mouth, any more than you could a Mexican cannons. They never have no disease that a good club won't heal.

If they ever die they must come rite tew life again, for i never heard nobody say "ded mule."

They are like some men, very corrupt at heart; I've known them tew be good mules for 6 months, just tew git a good chanse to kick somebody.

I never owned one, nor never mean to, unles there is a United Staits law passed, requiring it.

The only reason why they are patient, is because they are ashamed ov themselfs.

I have seen educated mules in a circus.

They could kick, and bite, tremenjis. I would not say what I am forced to say again the mule, if his birth want an outrage, and man want tew blame for it.

Any man who is willing tew drive a mule, ought to be exempt by law from running for the legislature.

They are the strongest creaturs on earth, and heaviest according tew their size; i heard tell ov one who fell off from the tow path, on the Erie kanawl, and sunk as soon as he touched bottom, but he kept rite on towing the boat tew the next station, breathing thru his ears, which stuck out ov the water about 2 feet 6 inches; i did'nt see this did, but an auctioneer told me ov it, and i never knew an auctioneer tu lie unless it was absolutely convenient.

That joke made me feel good as a pig in a hog-waller.

KORN

Korn iz a serial, i am glad ov it.

It got its name from Series, a primitive woman, and in her day, the goddess ov oats, and such like.

Korn iz sometimes called *maize*, and it grows in some parts of the western country, very amazenly.

I have seen it out there 18 foor hi (i dont mean the actual korn itself, but the tree on which it grows.)

Korn haz ears, but never has but one ear, which iz az deaf az an adder.

Injun meal iz made out ov korn, and korn dodgers iz made out ov injun meal, and korn dodgers are the tuffest chunks, ov the bread persuasion, known tew man.

Korn dodgers are made out ov water, with injun meal mixed into it, and then baked on a hard board, in the presence ov a hot fire.

When yu can't drive a 10 penny nail into them, with a sledge hammer, they are said, by good judges, to be well done, and are ready tew be chawed upon.

I have gnawed two hours myself on one side of a korn dodger without producing any result, and i think i could starve to death twice before i could seduce a korn dodger.

The get the name *dodger* from the immediate necessity ov dodgeing, if one iz hove horizontally at you in anger.

It iz far better tew be smote bi a 3-year-old steer, than a korn dodger, that iz only three hours old.

Korn was fust discovered by the injuns, but where they found it i don't know, and i don't know as i care.

Whiskey (noble whiskey) is made our ov korn, and whiskey is one ov the greatest blessings known tew man.

We never should have bin able tew fill our state prisons with energetic men, and our poor-houses with good eaters, if it want for noble whiskey.

We never should have had any temperance sons ov society, nor democratic pollyticians, nor prize fights, nor good murders, nor phatt aldermen, nor whiskey rings, nor nothing, if it want for blessed whiskey.

If it want for korn, how could any boddy git korned?

And if it want for gitting korned, what would like be worth?

We should all sink down to the level ov the brutes if it want for gitting korned.

The brutes don't git korned, they haint got any reason nor soul.

We often hear ov "*drunken brutes*," this is a compliment to oxen which dont belong tew them.

Korn also haz kernels, and kernels are often korned, so are brigadier-ginerals.

Johnny cake is made out ov korn, so iz hasty pudding.

Hasty pudding and milk is quick tew eat.

All you have got to do iz to gap, and swallow, and that iz the last ov the pudding.

Korn waz familiar tew antiquity. Joseph was sent down into Egypt after sum korn, but his brothers didn't want him to go, so they took pity on him and pitted him in a pit.

When his brothers got back home, and were asked where Joe waz, they didn't acknowledge the korn, but lied sum.

It has been proved, that it iz wicked to lie about korn, or any ov the other vegetables.

There iz this difference between lying, and sawing wood, it iz easier to lie, especially in the shade.

Korn has got one thing that nobody else has got, and that iz a kob.

This kob runs the middle ov the korn, and iz as phull ov korn as Job waz ov boils.

I always feel sorry when i think ov Job, and wonder how he managed tew set down in a chair.

Knowing how tew set down, square on a boil, without hurting the chair, iz one ov the lost arts.

Job was a card, he had more patience and boils, tew the square inch, than iz usual.

One hundred and twenty-five acres ov korn tew the bushel iz considered a good crop, but i have seen more.

I hav seen korn sold for 10 cents a bushel, and in some parts of the western country, it iz so much, that there aint no good law against stealing it.

In conclusion, if you want tew git a sure crop ov korn, and a good price for the crop, feed about 4 quarts ov it to a shanghi rooster, then murder the rooster immediately, and sell him for 17 cents a pound, crop and all.

Abuse is the logic of loafers.

"Is this the 520 acres of gentle rolling pasture land that was advertised?"

He was plumb wore out pantin' an' limp as a wornout fiddle string. His pore head hangin' down like a neck-wrung rooster's.

A Texan, a hard-bitten cattleman, lucked into it when they found a wealth of oil on his ranch. He built a magnificent home with luxuriant grounds, stables, guest houses and three swimming pools. One old friend who visited him asked why he needed three huge swimming pools.

"Well, I like to please all my friends," the Texan replied. "So

I fill one pool with cold water, the other with warm water and the third pool stays empty."

"Did I hear you right? One for cold, one for warm, one for empty?"

"Yep."

"But why the empty pool?"

"Skeeter, old buddy. You'd be amazed how many of my old friends can't swim a lick."

That old boy wasn't takin' no chances. He was about as cautious as a prostitute at confession.

Priscilla Jean came home on the train from her first year at Vasser College, got into the family car with her father and said to him. "Pa, I aim to tell you the truth. You deserve that much and I never kept anything from you. Don't intend to begin now.

"Pa, I . . . I . . . I ain't a good girl any more."

The father clapped his hand to his brow and moaned: "Twenty years your Ma and I been amakin' sacrifices so's you could git to college and make somethin' of yourself. And then what happens! Ya come home and danged if you ain't still sayin' 'ain't.' "

Let me tell you, buddy, that once she'd caught him he was plumb lady-broke.

There are four kinds of bulls, the beef cattle farmer informed a visitor on his farm. One kind wants to go to Rome and become a Papal bull. The other kind wants to go ceramic and become a bull in a china shop.

Yet a third type of bull would go to Wall Street and become a big shot competing against the Bears. And the last kind is an old stick-in-the-mud because he wants to stay in the pasture for heifer and heifer and heifer.

He's busier than a cat in the fish department.

A reporter visited a farmer, the third generation on the same home place. He noticed an old man scooping silage out of a trench and asked who he was. "That's my Pa. He's ninety years old."

"Is he in good health."

"Naw, he's showin' poorly of late."

"What's wrong with him?"

"Danged if I know. Sometimes I think farmin' don't agree with him."

I was so wore out that it took me all night to do what I used to do all night.

He lived the kind of life as would have made them murder mysteries look like a new testament.

As the nation was coming out of the depression in the 1930s, President Hoover complained to Calvin Coolidge: "I just don't understand why the American people don't cheer my new recovery program."

Calvin Coolidge replied: "Don't be in such a hurry. You can't see results the day after you turn the bull in with the cows."

"Well," said Hoover, "Maybe not. But I expect to see contented cows!"

I been eatin' so much pork that I'm sweating straight leaf lard.

A farmer had complained for years that scientists ought to leave Mother Nature alone. "That old girl knows what she's adoin'," he said. "She's been at it billions of years and these pipsqueak scientists got no business changin' her style."

"Now what's happened?" he was asked.

"Those dern fools have discovered somethin' beside whiskey to treat an ordinary cold, that's what."

I don't know where you come by this whiskey but whoever give or sold it to you musta had kidney trouble.

———————

The telephone company forgot and left in the hog pen, a keg of dynamite. One of the hogs managed to pry open the keg and proceeded to eat the dynamite. Then the hog wandered into the barn where the mule kicked him and the dynamite exploded. Well, that killed the mule, completely demolished the barn and every window in the farmer's house. The bell in the Methodist church, three miles away, pealed for half an hour from the concussion and vibrations.

The farmer reported that for over a week he had a mighty sick hog on his hands.

———————

Things was sure tough. Why even the buffalo on the nickel was gettin' thin.

———————

The Sunday sermon went on endlessly as the preacher exhorted his congregation to mend their ways. He used example after example, made point after point, quoted biblical passage after passage. At last he sighed: "What more can I say?" he queried the congregation.

A voice from the rear sung out, "Say 'Amen!' "

———————

There once was a cow named Bernadine.
Who loved to jump on a trampoline.
She once did give milk.
That was just smooth as silk.
But now she gives only whipped cream.

———————

Listen feller, you better talk straight! You jest grab thet bull by the tail and look the matter square in the face.

———————

"You can talk about your modern sickles all you want," the farmer argued with his neighbors at the town cafe. "But I still use my old John Deere I bought in 1960. Yep! Why, I go to the field to mow with it and I don't have to so much as start the power take-off or release. I just pass over a 7' width of alfalfa and the shadow of that sickle is enough to cut a swath!"

That joke is about as funny as a fart in a space suit!

There was a farmer named Billie,
whose walk was sillier than silly,
'cause one leg was far shorter
by an inch and a quarter,
Because they guy's farm was so hilly.

He fell off his mental reservation and ain't gone back since.

Out in Utah they tell the story of the sheep rancher who all his life wanted a fine car. So he went to the bank, borrowed enough money to buy himself a classy Cadillac limousine. Weeks later, the salesman called him on the telephone and asked how he liked the new car.

"It's a dandy," the rancher told him. "OK in every way. But I especially like that glass partition you talked me into buying. I admit I figured it was an extravagance but I sure like it now."

"Yeah?" murmured the bemused salesman. "Why?"

"When I bring the sheep in from pasture, the glass keeps 'em from lickin' my neck."

He told yarns, lies that were long as a whore's dream.

Perhaps the best answer as to why cowboys want to die with their boots on was given by a youngster: "I always figured," he said, "that they needed their boots on so's not to hurt their feet when they kicked the bucket."

The Dean of the School of Agriculture was interviewing a

new student and asked him why he wanted to go into farming.

"I dream of making a million dollars in farming, just like my father," the student replied.

The dean was impressed. "Your father made a million dollars in farming?"

"On no," replied the student, "but he always dreamed of it!"

"Sure corn prices are terrible, but look at the bright side—
you had a poor crop!"

With permission of *Country Magazine*

He's so dang tight he gets out of bed to turn over so as not to wear out the sheets.

Everybody knows that the great Paul Bunyan and his blue ox, Babe, dredged the ditch for what we know as the Mississippi River; and plowed out the curves when they got too numerous or sharp. Well, such men are by no means finished, the line still goes on. Ivan Downing of Dagsboro, Delaware tells about his Grandpa:

"Back in my grandfather's day," Ivan alleges, "many rural roads followed old, winding Indian trails, and motorists found the sharp curves difficult to negotiate.

"Granddad decided to take matters into his own hands with the road he lived on. He drove some iron stakes into the end of the road, rigged up pulleys and levers, hooked up his team of horses—and yanked the road out straight!

"That's not all. When word got out about what he'd done, the county and township highway departments kept Granddad busy straightening other roads.

"Like a true country person, he refused to take any money for his work. But there was usually a little road left over after each had been straightened . . . and he kept those to sell as private drives!"

That feller is upholstered with more brains than a sheep dog.

We must mention the city farmer who dressed his scarecrow in an old tuxedo he had no need for in the country.

"How did it work?" inquired an observant neighbor.

"It didn't protect the corn any better," replied the city fellow, "but it attracted a better class of crows."

That rancher lives so far out on the prairie that sunlight has to be piped to him every blamed mornin'.

The speaker at the county Farm Bureau picnic had been on the platform far too long, and his audience had become inattentive and started chatting among themselves. He kept rambling on even though no one was listening.

Exasperated, the speaker interrupted his talk and turned to the chairman. "Mr. Chairman," he complained, "there are so many people talking in the audience that I can barely hear myself talk."

"Oh, that's all right," the chairman assured him. "You're not missing a thing!"

That old boy was plumb weak once you got past his ears headed north.

Years ago a Vermonter moved west to homestead some fertile ground in North Dakota, and he did well. He never returned to Vermont, but years later, Pete, one of his sons, did journey back where he visited with relatives.

A cousin about his own age showed the Dakotan his small barn and stony hillside farm. After looking it all over, the visitor said, "I really don't see how you manage to make a living here on these little farms. I should think you'd have starved to death by now."

"Jake," his host answered, "I expect we probably would starve, it we didn't have the interest we get on our North Dakoty mortgages!"

When old Jake challenged Pete you could jest tell that Pete was as nervous as a whore in church.

An Amish Farmer sold a horse and buggy to a non-Amish neighbor, with assurances that the horse was well trained.

"The one thing I should tell you," the Amishman said, "is that you must say 'Praise the Lord' to make him go, and to stop him you must say 'The Lord is my shepherd'."

The neighboring farmer nodded, climbed into the buggy and yelled "Praise the Lord!" The horse took off at a gallop.

Down the road a few miles, however, the farmer realized that he'd forgotten what to say to stop the animal—and the horse was racing toward a muddy pond! The farmer tried every Bible verse he could think of, all the while pulling back on the reins.

Just a few feet from the pond, the farmer finally remembered and yelled out, "The Lord is my shepherd!" The horse came to a halt just inches from the muddy bank.

Relieved that he'd avoided a good soaking, the farmer looked skyward and exclaimed, "Praise the Lor—" *Splash!*

He kinda took an unschedooled flight off'n that hoss.

Two veteran farmers, who had been through the ups and

downs of several decades, were asked what they would do if a million dollars were given them tomorrow.

"Why, I'd quit working, go fishing and take life easy," one replied.

"Not me," said the other. "I reckon I'd just keep on farming till the million was all gone."

Sure I know John. We acted horse at a Halloween party where I took the head and he took what came naturally for him.

What you see often depends on where you've been . . . and what you've lived through. Mary S. Wiley of Bethany, Oklahoma tells of a Texas rancher who well remembered the Dust Bowl days. One year he visited his grown son in California.

Overjoyed to see his father, the son took him to see all of California's many attractions, then—as a final treat—showed him the Pacific Ocean.

The old rancher stood looking at the water for a long time, not saying a word. Finally, his son asked, "What do you think of it, Dad?"

"Well, son," the awed rancher whispered back, "it sure would water a *big* herd of cattle!"

There ain't no use askin' him to be a nice guy. He just don't do imitations.

The circus parade had no sooner pulled into the small town when the strong man heard of a local farmer known for his feats of strength. Anxious to prove his superior muscle power, the strong man borrowed a circus horse and rode out to the farmer's place for a showdown.

"Hey, I've heard a lot about you!" the strong man yelled when he spotted the farmer in his fields. Getting off his horse and looking over the short, thin man, he added, "You sure don't look like much to me!"

With that, the farmer picked him up with one hand and threw him over the fence. When the circus strong man had finally regained his breath, the farmer looked at him and asked, "Is there anything else you want to say to me?"

"No, I guess not," the strong man replied. "But would you be good enough to toss me my horse?"

So he goes and applies to be a salesman, the darn fool. Why he couldn't sell hack-saw blades in a hoosegow.

"Is it true," a visitor asked an experienced cattleman, "that a mad bull won't hurt you if you carry a flashlight?"

"Yes, I guess so," replied the cattleman thoughtfully. "If you carry it fast enough."

He wants to better himself. So he's studyin' to be a half-wit.

His mother could hardly restrain naughty Johnny who kept getting into mischief all day. Toward mid-afternoon, when Mother was about to drop him down the well, Johnny came up with a solution. "Give me a quarter and I'll be good."

"Give you a quarter!" his mother exploded. "Why Johnny you shouldn't ask for money to be good. You should be just like your father . . . good for nothing."

He's crooked enough to sleep on a corkscrew.

Two farmers were in debt to the local banker. To quiet him and get him off their back, they invited him to go fishing in the adjoining farm pond. He accepted and they started out in the rowboat only to have it capsize in the middle of the pond. The farmers could swim but the banker couldn't. He was thrashing about helplessly when one of the farmers called to him: "Keep trying—can you float alone?"

The banker gasped: "I'm drowning and you want to talk business!"

He just hunkered down in that saddle tighter'n you could stick a postage stamp.

Old Doctor Tom Masters sat in the kitchen of the farmhouse, slowly sipping coffee. He had just delivered the 12th baby in fifteen years, all to the same family in the same house.

"You know, Doc, we've had so many kids that I've plumb run out of names. Danged if I know what to call this one."

Old Doc Masters put down his cup, thought a minute and said, "If I were you, I'd call it quits."

So I told the yeller coward, "Mister, go hunt you up something that'll do you for backbone."

The preacher came to the farm to visit Grandpa Thomas on his 93rd birthday. Grandpa admitted that he hadn't long to live and would soon be facing his Maker.

"How does that make you feel, Grandpa?" the pastor asked. "Can you face God with a clear conscience?"

"Well, Pastor, it's kinda like this: I know I've done a whale of a lot of things I hadn't oughta done. On the other hand, I ain't done a whale of a lot of things I oughta done. Now wouldn't you say that kinda evens things up?"

Every time a pretty gal comes near our outfit it's as if the whole range was sufferin' from Cupid's Cramp.

A householder wrote to the agent of the county extension service and asked advice, as follows: "What would be good to plant in an area that gets hardly any rain, has rocky soil, receives only an hour of sun and has what seems to be ineradicable crabgrass?"

The agent wrote: "Have you thought about a flagpole?"

"Yes, we do have a manure spreader in that price range . . . right around the corner."

With permission of *Country Magazine*

You don't want to cross that old boy. Why, that's risky as walkin' on quicksand over hell.

To her fourth grade class the physical education teacher posed the question of good posture, how to acquire and keep it.

"Johnny," she asked the boy from the farm, "How does one acquire good posture?"

"Plant a good mixture of grasses and legumes, fertilize it and don't turn the cows in too soon," the farm kid responded.

Do I like farmin'? Buddy, when I'm in the field I'm as happy as a kitten in a creamery.

New England farmers are known for their shrewd habit of replying to a question by asking another question. Here's an example. "How's your wife?" a neighbor inquired. "Compared to what?" was the equivocal reply.

Crooked? Why, he's so crooked when he eats nails he spits out corkscrews.

Everyone has heard of the very democratic town meetings in New England. At one of them, a farmer arose and asked the moderator if he could ask a few pertinent questions.

"So long as they're pertinent," was the reply.

"All right, Mr. Moderator. Please turn to page thirty of the Town Record. Do you agree that it reads that it cost the town a hundred dollars for Jane Sawyer to have her illegitimate baby?"

The Moderator agreed that the amount and use was correct.

"Well then, Mr. Moderator, if you turn to page thirty-five, would you agree with the record that the town fined the young man responsible for the impregnation, one hundred and fifty dollars?"

Again the moderator agreed that the question was affirmatively answered.

"And now for my third question. Did the town not make a profit of fifty dollars on the transaction?"

"Yeah, I suppose you could say that," said the Moderator.

"And now for my fourth and last question. Mr. Moderator, ladies and gentlemen of the township, do you not think, as I do, that it might very well pay the town to breed her again?"

It was so dark that night that I couldn't find my nose with both hands.

A city lady visited a silver fox farm. She was enchanted with the beauty of the animals and kept exclaiming how charming, sweet and even endearing they were. On and on she gushed. Then she asked the fur farmer how many pelts they got each year from a fox.

"Well," the fur farmer replied. "Generally, we take only one pelt a year because, if we take more than that, it makes them foxes damned nervous."

When the Lord was pourin' in brains fer that feller, somebody musta juggled His arm.

During World War II, a salesman for U.S. War Bonds visited a farmer. They sat on a swing on the porch and the salesman described his purpose but soon saw that the farmer did not understand what he was saying and was, in fact, very hard of hearing.

"Surely you know there's a war on!" He now spoke loudly.

The farmer looked puzzled.

Even louder now, the salesman shouted: "You must have heard about the trouble at Pearl Harbor?"

The old man shrugged.

"The names Roosevelt and Churchill, do they mean anything to you?" And the salesman was now shouting his questions.

Again the farmer seemed not to have heard him. And so the salesman left for richer, easier pastures.

The farmer went back in the house and his wife asked him who that man was who shouted so much.

"Can't say as I rightly know," the farmer answered her.

"But if I heard him right, he was talkin' about some feller by the name of Rosyfelt. Seems this Rosyfelt got his girl, Pearl Harbor, in trouble over on Church Hill and the danged fool come way over here to ask me to go his bond!"

That fiddler was talkin' a special kinda language that put ginger in my feet.

A customer came to the still, far out in the hills, where the moonshiner made the best moonshine in the area. But this time he asked a higher price. Surprised, the customer inquired why he had asked so much more for the bottle than last time.

"It was a vintage ear," responded the moonshiner.

So I pulled outa that town figurin' that a change of pasture makes a fatter calf.

A traveler was hot and dusty when he came to a cool-looking farm pond. He stripped and jumped in to find the water wonderfully cooling. But when he decided to get out he noticed a very pretty young lady sitting on the bank, grinning at him. "Go away, please," the nude bather shouted. "I need to get out and go on my way and I can't with you sitting there." The girl just sat there grinning and happy as a hog swimming in corn meal mush.

The fellow felt a round, pan-like object beneath him, bent down and picked it out of the water, then placed it over his privates and marched out.

"Young woman, you know what I'm going to do?" the bather asked.

"Yep," the pretty girl said. "I'll bet you figure on welding a bottom to that dishpan you're holding."

His yellow streak was so wide it come clean around his backbone till it tickled his tit.

Three farm lads had been making fence for their father.

They were told that the telephone company wanted help in setting poles, so figuring that they had the know-how, they applied and were hired.

At the end of the first day, the boys were asked how many poles they had set. "Three," they replied triumphantly. But their faces fell when the boss told them they'd have to do a lot better.

The next evening they reported that they had set five posts. Again the boss was unhappy.

Because they set only six posts on the third day, the boss fired them.

Later the boss learned that the boys had left only five feet each of the telephone poles they'd set, sticking out of the ground!

Her feet was bout the size of a loading chute.

The farmer had increasing trouble providing for his thirteen kids. He told his wife that if she got pregnant again, why he'd just go shoot himself. Well, that fertile female did get pregnant again and the husband, as he'd promised, took his pistol and went behind the barn to eliminate half the problem.

A neighbor came by and asked to see the farmer. His wife, beside herself, told the visitor that her husband had taken a pistol and gone behind the barn to shoot himself.

The neighbor ran behind the barn and found the farmer leaning on a post, picking his teeth and contemplating distant horizons.

"I was afraid that you were gonna do yourself in, George," the neighbor told him.

"I planned to do just that," the farmer said. "But then I got to considerin' all angles and I figured that I just might be executing an innocent man."

Two small town friends met to discuss the recent death of the town's wealthiest (and stingiest) citizen. "How much money did old Bill leave?" the one man asked.

"All of it!"

That gal is so fat that when she fell in the river she dried up half a mile of it.

One evening, after his sermon, the pastor asked the members of his church to state what the Lord had done for them. Quite a few stood and told about received benefits and cures. Then one old man, obviously arthritic, bent and distorted with the disease, got up and made his declaration: "You want to know what the good Lord done fer me, do ya? Well, I'm agonna tell ya! He danged near ruint me, that's what!"

That ol' boy talks a good ride but he's all gargle and no guts.

There was one farmer-member of the country church who was known as the township skinflint. Whenever money was needed he refused to give. And they hadn't counted on him this particular Sunday when they were trying to raise money to repair the organ. Nor had the skinflint offered to give. Then a tiny piece of plaster fell on his head and he stood and said: "I pledge ten dollars."

A voice in the back of the church shouted: "Oh Lord, for our sakes, hit him again and harder!"

A feller who straddles a fence gets a sore crotch.

And then there is the stellar advice given by a father to his son who was going for his tryout with a professional baseball team. "Son, remember this," the old man said, "Don't ever hit a baseball player that chews tobacco."

There ain't nothing can mess up a good farmhand like that little feller with the bow and arrow.

In Southern Illinois, they tell the story of a poor dirt farmer who was approached by an oil company that proposed to drill on his farm. Leases were signed and all were in hopes of a rich strike. But, alas, it was a dry hole and the oil company began to move out. Just as they began to move the rig away from the hole, the farmer suggested that they use the equipment to move his outhouse and set it right over the drilled hole. "I've moved that danged outhouse five times to new holes," the farmer said. "You got a nice, deep one here and it'd oblige me if you'd just set my outhouse over it."

The drillers were glad to oblige and moved his privy over the deep shaft.

Next morning, the farmer's son came running to the barn, very excited. "I'm scared something's happened to Mama. She's asettin' in the outhouse and she doesn't look right. Her eyes is set hard and her face is turnin' blue and her eyes are all bugged out and her veins is all puffed out in her neck!"

"Nothin' to worry about, Sonny. Your Mama is just fine. She always did enjoy holding her breath till she hears it hit bottom."

He was jest 'bout as graceful on a hoss as an elephant is tryin' to use a typewriter.

The farmer brought some bonds to the bank and handed them over to the cashier.

"I need to know whether these are for redemption or conversion," the cashier asked.

"That all depends," the farmer said, grinning. "Is this the bank or the First Baptist Church?"

Howdy friend—light and have yourself a hog squat.

Old Joe Fleischer had been prone to drink too much. His good wife stayed with him and, finally, had Joe pretty much a teetotaler.

But one night Joe came home heavily "lit," and his poor wife, disgusted with him, said: "Joe Fleischer, you aren't going to sleep in this house tonight. Go to the barn." He went!

Deep in the night, Mrs. Fleischer awakened, felt remorse for what she had done, and went looking for Joe. He wasn't in the barn! Alarmed, she looked high and low and finally found him in the hog shed, nestled next to a sow.

"Joe, dear Joe, wake up and come to the house."

Joe stirred, rolled nearer the sow and began to run his hand over the sow's belly . . . "Jane, dear Jane. I don't recall you having that many buttons on the front of your nightgown."

You got no more chance than a one-legged mare at a kickin' contest.

"I'm here to learn about your grafting experiments!"

With permission of *Country Magazine*

There was once a teller of tall tales who came to town and told about the oil drilling going on at his farm. He said that the previous night a heckuva windstorm came along and blew the oil well clean out of the ground. But, with typical American ingenuity, they fixed things for the better. What did they do? "Well," the farmer said, "we took that blamed hole and cut it up into fenceposts, enough to fence my twenty acre, east pasture!"

That ol' feller never got past the flyleaf of a first grade primer!

Two elderly spinsters, with a lifetime on the farm, were discussing what, if they had their druthers, they'd like to have in a man. "Brains," said the one lady. "He's got to have brains."

"Not for me," replied the other. "I count more on appearances. And the sooner the appearance the better!"

He was helpless as a man tryin' to scratch his ear with his elbow.

He's as restless as a short-tailed bull in flytime.

"Look! There's the colossal old boar, now!"

With permission of *Country Magazine*

At the Missouri State Fair, a farmer challenged a sword swallower to perform his act outside the tent, without props. The performer agreed, grabbed a handful of nails and swallowed them. "Hold on there," yelled the farmer. "Them nails ain't swords. You cheated."

He said he was throwed so high he shook hands with St. Peter 'fore he started down.

———————

Can you guess what Noah's wife said to Noah when they pulled up the anchor and began their cruise? One hint: she was worried about the termites aboard. No? Give up? Well, Mrs. Noah said, "Y'know, Noah, I'd feel a lot easier in my mind if you'd lock those termites in a metal box."

———————

That feller was so conceited he had callouses from pattin' hisself on the back.

———————

It is said that the following philosophical observation was inserted in the *Congressional Record*, in 1940: "Some people tell us that there ain't no hell. But they never farmed, so how can they tell!"

———————

That hoss threw him clean into a funeral parlor.

———————

It takes one (farmer) to know one. Pope John came from a farm background so that he knew exactly what he was saying, knew from experience when he remarked: "People go to ruin in three ways—women, gambling and farming. My family chose the slowest one!"

———————

Dwight D. Eisenhower used to love to tell this story. It is easy to see why. But Mark Twain told the story first.

There was once a farmer who aspired to his Missouri State Legislature and wanted to be elected more than anything he had ever wanted before. Feeling inferior about his lack of a college education, he tried to make up for it by using every big word he could think of. As a result, his speeches were hard to understand and almost impossible to follow. He wasn't doing well, votewise.

One evening at home and milking the family cow, the cow

kicked him in the face causing him to bite off the end of his tongue. It seemed that the young farmer's political career was at an end.

The young man continued his campaign and, as Mark Twain put it, "after that he could use only words of one syllable, and it made his speeches so simple and appealing to the farmers that he was elected and re-elected term after term.

That dude'll fight a buzz saw and give it ten revolutions.

There is an old story that goes back to those stubborn mule days. And the moral of it is so useful that it bears repeating. It seems that the farmer bought a mule, took it home, put it in its traces but the mule balked, simply would not move no matter how much the farmer yelled, pushed and shoved. So he took it back to the dealer. The dealer again put the mule in traces and tried to get it to move, but it balked.

"You see! That's the trouble. That mule is too balky to work."

Just then the dealer picked up a big hedge post and hit the mule, bringing it to its knees. The mule staggered upright, shook its head and proceeded to follow the dealer's commands from then on.

"What . . . what the heck did you do?" the buyer asked.

"Well, y'see, first you've got to get a mule's attention," the dealer explained. "After that they work real well."

There is a wonderful story that farmers and ranchers enjoy ...but their wives detest. Here it goes. It seems that a farmer, long ago, married on a Sunday morning and, after the ceremonies, put his bride in the buggy and started off toward their new home. Suddenly, once out of sight of the church, the horse balked. No words could get that horse moving.

The groom stepped out of the buggy, walked to the front to stand before the horse and said: "That's once!" Then he hit the horse between the eyes so hard it fell to its knees. Slowly it staggered to its feet. The groom walked to the wagon, mounted and said: "Giddyap," and the horse started as nice as you please.

The new bride said nothing.

About a mile on down the road the horse balked again. This time the groom walked to the horse and said: "That's twice!" Then he hit the horse so hard, the beast lay stunned for several minutes. Slowly, slowly, the horse got to it feet. Once again beside his bride, the groom clucked the horse onward at a good pace.

But it was not to last. For the third time the horse balked. Fortunately, they were within easy walking distance of their new home. But this time the groom took a pistol from under the wagon seat, walked to the front of the horse, and said, "That's three times!" He then shot the horse dead. Walking around to his bride, he reached up his hand to help her down. But she refused. "That, sir, was the most brutal thing I have ever witnessed! If I had known how cruel you were . . . if I had known . . . oh!"

The groom stood there a moment, then said—pointing his finger at her—"That's once!"

She wasn't wearin' enough clothes to dust a fiddle.

A Kentucky farmer won a trip to the Hawaiian Islands. On his return, his friends wanted to know all about his experiences. One of them asked if he'd seen a hula dancer.

"Yep," the returned vacationer told them, "I sure did. The dance goes like this. First she ties a string of rice stalks around her middle and then she dangles shredded sugar cane from the rice stalks all around her and she finishes with a lot of pineapple tops strung around that. Then, when she's got it all planted, she rotates the crops."

It was so cold the cow let down icicles.

Two farmers were walking down State Street in Chicago

when they noticed an odd apparition walking toward them. It was a woman whose fingernails were painted bright red, her hair pushed up in an enormous bouffant, all kinds of reds and whites went to make up her complexion and to top it off she had her lips done in bright red.

"Wow! Ain't that somethin'," exclaimed one fellow.

"All I can say," said his buddy, "is this. Only godawful poor soil would need all that top dressing!"

He was one of them jerks who figure the sun comes up jest to hear him crow.

A young boy, on his first visit to that same big and windy city of Chicago, was fascinated by a woman coming toward him holding on to her wide-brimmed hat while the wind pushed her skirts higher and higher up her legs. She noticed the lad.

"Young man," she said as she passed him, "what you were looking at is forty years old but what I'm holding onto is brand new."

The pore old feller finally give up, saddled a cloud and rode up to visit Saint Peter,

---

Dame Barker had a
    Yerling hen
Who swore she'd set,
    or raise the dickens;
The dame sot her on an ear ov corn
    and raised a bushul
and a half of chickens.
    (Josh Billings: 1818–1888)

He had on a dude outfit that was shore splendiferous.

The crochety old farmer lay in his hospital bed shivering.

He saw a nurse pass and yelled to her. "Nurse! Nurse! My feet feel like two cakes of ice. Would you please bring me a hot-water bottle?"

The nurse stopped, came into the room and fixed him with a haughty glare. "Sir! If . . . you . . . please! I'm the head nurse."

"All right. All right. So call me the foot nurse!"

So he gives with a stud horse whistle that'd pull the pin of every filly near here.

The rancher was very sick. His doctor stood looking down on the sick man. "Mr. Jones. I must be honest with you. You are a very sick man. You'll never leave the hospital. Now, sir, is there anyone you would like me to call in your last moments?"

"Yes, SIR! Mr. Doctor. Ah sho would appreciate it if y'all would call me anothuh doctuh."

That old boy caught him a bullet in his belly he couldn't digest. So we put him to bed with a pick and shovel.

Two farmers were sitting around the general store commiserating on the damage the potato bugs had done to their potatoes.

"In just ten days them derned bugs et my entire potato crop," one farmer moaned.

"Ten days," remarked the other farmer. "It took 'em ten days? Why, them pesky critters et mine in just two days and then roosted up in my big oak tree to see if I was going to plant some more."

Then the store owner said: "That's mild compared to what I got goin' on right now, back in my office. Why there's three of them bugs goin' through my books to see who has ordered seed potatoes for next spring."

He kept his foot on the brass rail so much it danged near took root.

An old rancher was eating dinner in a fancy French restaurant in Denver. The waiter was making a great ceremony of creating crepes suzette. At the climactic moment, as required, the entire dish burst into flames.

"They ain't servin' vittles here. Appears to me they're fixin' to shoe a horse!"

"Hello, farm supply?
About that weed killer that you sold me . . . "

When you ride, keep one leg firm on each side and yore mind in the middle.

Next is the story of two farmers who were a little bit deaf. Each one could hear, but each was just deaf enough that he could never hear anything quite right.

One day they were taking a cross-country trip in their pickup truck. As they passed through a strange town, one said, "What town is this?"

"Wellesley,"

"Wednesday? Oh, I thought it was Thursday."

"So am I. Let's stop and have a drink!"

———————

Little Johnny, a city boy in the country for the first time, saw the milking of a cow.

"Now you know where the milk comes from, don't you?" he was asked.

"Sure!" replied Johnny. "You give the cow some breakfast food and water, and then drain the crankcase."

———————

That farm hand of mine couldn't follow a load of hay across a field of snow.

———————

I was in the checkout line of a hardware store in Illinois. The young man in front of me had an assortment of vegetable seeds and garden supplies. "How's the farm coming along?" the clerk asked, trying to start up a conversation.

"Not bad."

She tried again. "How's the new baby?"

"Better," he said.

"Oh, has she been sick?" the clerk persisted.

"Nope," he said. "Just better than the farm."

Mrs. Vera MacGillivray, Clinton

———————

In Texas they have enormous theatres (of course), so big that when a cowboy in the last row throws an egg at a lousy actor, it hatches before it hits the stage. But then everything is that big in Texas—except modesty.

———————

Some folks can't drink. Givin' 'em likker is like tryin' to play a harp with a hammer.

———————

When farmers once debated the respective merits of horses and tractors, a city fellow stopped by the fence to chat with a farmer plowing with a team in the field by the road.

"My good man," the fellow asked, "why are you still using horses in this machine age?"

"Machines don't last," the farmer replied. "You have to keep buying new ones every few years."

"Well," the city man said, "I suppose your horses don't wear out?"

"Yep. I reckon they will," the farmer nodded. "But before I'm through with these mares, they'll give me a new replacement."

That feller's head is so hollow he's gotta talk with his hands to git away from the echo.

Neighbors were puzzled when Ed, a retired farmer in eastern Nebraska just past his 80th birthday, came home from Omaha with a bride in her early 30's—Ed's junior by nearly half a century.

When someone asked Ed why he hadn't chosen a wife more nearly his own age, Ed thought a bit and then replied. "Well, the fact is, I like the smell of perfume better than liniment."

Was he fast? Well I guess! That ol' boy could move faster'n a deacon takin' up a collection.

There once was a bull who was fated
To see all his lady friends mated.
Off they would prance
Without even a glance—
Artificially inseminated!

Glenna Henderson of Tower City, North Dakota

They was friends, all right, close enough to use the same toothpick.

One rainy summer day, Pete Jones from Southern Illinois was having difficulty plowing a field on his farm. Finally his tractor became so deeply mired that he had to go back for tools to extricate it. A neighbor, seeing him struggling to extricate the heavy tractor, called out, "You having a little trouble, Pete?"

"Not hardly," Pete grinned. "Trouble is somethin' I cain't fix."

He shore was pleased an' grinnin' jest like a weasel peekin' in a henhouse door.

An Oklahoma rancher was complaining about the drought. "Even the creek, my old standby for water, dried up."

"Well, when it was runnin', why didn't you dam it?" the storekeeper asked.

"I did. I damned the hell out of it but cussin' never helped a raindrop's worth."

You call it lightning but I tell ya it's that Old Man up there stompin' out his campfire and asettin' the sparks a-flyin'.

It was a boiling hot day, 100° plus. And old Aaron was rocking away on his front porch while his wife was pulling weeds in the garden. "Isn't that awful hard work for Mama on such a hot day?" his small son asked.

"Good point, son," old Aaron said. "B'lieve I'll just tell Mama to come inside and do the house chores."

It was so hot that I blowed one solid hour on a cup of coffee and still it was too hot to drink.

A Tennessee farmer couldn't make farming pay so he

turned to making moonshine. He was caught red-handed and hauled into court for the fifth time!

"Before passing sentence," the Judge sternly told the prisoner, "I want to say that you've given this court more trouble than any other person in the entire state of Tennessee."

"Judge, let me say this. I ain't givin' you any more trouble than you been givin' me."

There was plenty of hell to pave after that . . . and no hot tar.

The rancher rises early in the morning, knows what he has to do, straddles his hoss and gets to work. He does his best and spends little.

The politician gets up late, straddles the fence, spends all our money and *then* decides what to do.

It sure don't take no backbone to belly up to a bar.

An old nester who was never known to do a lick of work always showed up at the neighboring ranch chuck wagon at branding time. He got a full meal this way. He tried to help but he was in the way so much he was more trouble than he was worth. It got so that when the old feller rode up, the cowboys would say: "Here comes Jim. When he arrives, it's just like two good men leavin'."

He said he was hungrier than a woodpecker with a headache.

Back in the old days, before modern conveniences like the telephone became ordinary as sunlight, a farmer, in town, decided to try the telephone at the store. He called the home where his wife was visiting. Just as his wife answered a bolt of lightning hit the telephone line and knocked the farmer "ass over end."

When he recovered and his head cleared, he remarked: "That's her, for sure!"

That weaklin' is so hen-pecked he moults at least once a year.

An old rancher, none too bright, was after many years talked into seeing his first movie. He watched it with little interest until a group of beautiful girls started to undress . . . to go swimming. Of course, censorship required that something in the movie, such as a train, must pass by to shield their nudity. And the next scene showed them in the water.

The old fellow sat there through three shows until a curious usher asked him why he remained through so many performances.

"Well," the old boy answered, "I aim to sit here until that dern train is late!"

"I just bought a lifetime supply of fresh fertilizer!"

That old feller looked as unhappy as a motherless calf. He his kindlin' gettin' his fire started.

said he had more troubles than Job had boils. I figured him to be about as miserable as a woodpecker in a petrified forest.

"Stress?" the farmer said in answer to how he would define the word. "Stress is a kind of confusion that comes over me when my mind says 'no' to my body wanting to choke the livin' daylights out of some asshole who positively, certainly, undoubtedly sure as hell needs it."

He was about as useless as tits on a boar hog, or settin' a milk pail under a bull. Why expectin' work out of him was like expectin' tail lights on Noah's ark. Hirin' him was as useless as if you was to salt the ocean.

A rich bachelor rancher died leaving a will that read as follows:

"To my cousin George, I leave my cattle. To my faithful cook and housekeeper, Tanzia, I leave my house and entire ranch acreage. And to my nephew, Strongfellow, who always argued with me that health means more than wealth, I leave my saddle, bridal, tennis racquet and golf clubs."

He was a nice enough feller but lazy, always sittin' around on his end-gate.

A successful famer was interviewed by the weekly newspaper. He was asked if he could tell readers to what he owed his success. He told about an old rooster he had observed on his father's farm.

"This rooster could peck harder, jump faster, fly higher and fight better than any other rooster in the place. But he lost most of his fights, even against punier roosters. The trouble was that just as he was winning a fight, he would stop to crow."

He's a shrewd ol' boy, all right. You won't catch him usin' all

A male cow is known as a bull—that they breed in Oklahoma, butcher in Missouri, fight in Mexico and shoot in Texas.

He was showin' off and struttin' about like a turkey gobbler in a hen pen.

Chicken makes a marvelous food. But you can feed too much of it as in this Arizona case. The lady fed her kids so much chicken that they got rid of the mattresses and took to roostin' on the springs.

He was some sick, all right. He was sufferin' like a centipede with sore feet.

Two Wisconsin farmers were discussing the recent death of a neighbor.
"Did he have anything to say, there at the last?" one farmer asked.
"Not hardly. His wife was with him till he died."

She loved to sing. And loud! But she sounded like a long-drawn squeak of a slow runnin' windmill jest acryin' for grease. Her songs was kinda weak on melody but strong as all git out on noise.

The Ford Motor Company is said to have received this terse, telling note from an R.F.D. box:
"Gentlemen:
I understand you made a complete car in three minutes. The newspaper here had an article on it. Now, if you need proof, I can give it because I got that car!"

That hill road was slicker'n snot on a door knob.

An old couple sat on the porch rocking gently and saying nothing. After hours of this silent rocking, Maybelle asked: "George, is it raining?"

George put his hand beyond the porch railing, then said, "Nope."

In silence the rocking went on for another hour, then: "George, has it started to rain yet?"

George again put his hand beyond the railing, withdrew it and said, "Nope!"

After another hour of absolute quiet and rocking, Maybelle asked: "George whatever happened to our marital relations?"

George replied: "Ain't they telephoned recently?"

––––––––––

He's kind of a stay-at-home. Goin' around the coffee pot lookin' fer the handle would cover the extent of his travelin'.

––––––––––

The young lady rushed to the reception desk at the hospital. "Yes?" inquired the nurse on duty.

"I want to see an upturn!"

"I think you mean intern, Miss."

"Uptern, intern, I got to get a contamination."

"I think you mean examination, Miss."

"Contamination, examination, so what! It's a testicle I got to have."

"Dear me, Miss! You must mean a test?"

"All right, so it's test, so it's examination and even intern. The point I got to make is . . . I haven't demonstrated in three months and I think I'm stagnant!"

––––––––––

Confused? Well, somewhat! Why that old girl couldn't find her own butt in a privy.

––––––––––

The tourist, not sure of where he was, saw an old fellow standing by the country road. He drove to him, stopped the car and, before asking direction, queried the old man: "Do you live around here?"

"Yep."

"Have you lived here all your life?"

"Not yit!"

He's long in the tooth and don't travel like a colt no more but, like a steer, he still tries.

Shorty Elliot had bought cars from a dealer in the town nearest him and, always, he had been peeved at the extras tacked onto the list price by the dealer. So when the dealer needed a cow for his family, naturally he came to the farm of his good customer, Shorty Elliott.

The dealer picked out a very nice cow and asked the price.

"That's a two-hundred-dollar cow," Shorty replied.

"Good enough. I'll take her." He took out his checkbook.

"That's the basic price," Shorty cautioned him. "There are a couple of extras, of course." He whipped out a pad and pencil and began to figure. Finished, he handed the slip to the dealer and here is what was written on it:

Basic cow	$ 200.00
Brown, black and white exterior	50.00
Four stomachs at $25 apiece	100.00
Genuine, all-leather cowhide seat covers	80.00
Two horns, $10 each	20.00
Automatic fly-swatter	40.00
Four faucets for refreshments at $7 each	28.00
Storage area and dispensing equipment	50.00
	$560.00

That ol' boy left home in such a hurry he forgot to take his right name along. Y' see, his name didn't exactly tally with the one fer him wrote in the Bible.

Texas is unbelievably vast. They tell about the land-hungry

family back in pioneer days who started out from Texarkana in east Texas to homestead in El Paso. The had one baby. Now, that state of Texas is so large that by the time the family reached the homestead, their baby was chewin' tobacco and rolling his own cigarettes.

That Texas dude was so tough that when he heaved a sigh on the east side of town you could feel the draft on the west side. When he chewed nails he spit tacks! Dangerous? He's dangerouser than a loaded skunk. His eyes were somethin' else . . . why they'd chill a danged lamb and a side of beef.

"About how short do you like 'em, Mac?"

A woman came running into the doctor's office dragging a small boy behind her. "Doctor! Doctor! He needs help! He swallowed a .22 bullet. Oh my, what'll I do?"

The doctor quieted her and told her it wasn't all that serious. Then he handed her a bottle. "It's castor oil," he said. "Now you take the boy home and feed him the entire bottle . . . but there's one thing you must not do . . . don't aim him at anybody."

That kid made me nervous as a longtailed cat under a rockin' chair.

A farmer wrote to Montgomery Ward: Dear M & W: would you please send me three sacks of corn cobs. Payment enclosed."

Montgomery Ward wrote back: "Dear Sir: If you look on page 42 of our latest catalogue you will note that we no longer stock this item."

The farmer wrote back: "Dear M & W: Dangit all, anyway! If I had your catalogue I wouldn't need the cobs! Thank you."

The feedlot smelled worse than hell on house-cleanin' day.

The rancher moved his outhouse to a new location quite a ways from the ranch house. But he didn't cover the hole because it was growing too dark to see.

That night, Grandpa needed to use the facilities and went out to relieve himself. But he fell in the hole, up to his chest, and couldn't climb out. "FIRE! FIRE!" he yelled at the top of his voice.

The folks all came running, pulled him out, hosed him clean and took him back to the house, relieved that there was no fire. "But Grandpa!" his son asked. "Why in heck did you holler 'fire'?"

"I figured that if I hollered 'shit,' who in heck would bother to come help me?"

That feller smelled worse than a sheepherder's socks. I couldn't stand to git close enough to borrow a chaw. Yep! He was some whiffy on the lee side.

The lad was courting the neighboring farmer's daughter. Now, he'd baked beans for supper and was full of gas yet embarrassed to relieve himself of it. So he fidgeted and squirmed and was beside himself until he thought of the piano. Walking quickly to it he began to play a piece he announced was entitled "THE DELUGE."

The music helped enormously because every time he had to break wind he would play fortissimo, loud as hell, as if the storm had broken loose and thunder and lightning was everywhere.

When he finished he asked how she liked the famous piece.

"I liked it just fine," the girl said, grinning. "But if you play it again—and I'd like to hear it once more—just leave out that part where the lightning hit the shithouse."

———————————

Come on in and line yore flue with some good thunderberries. They'll feed yore tapeworm good.

———————————

The farm wife used half a bottle of naptha doing her spring cleaning. Faced with storing it or throwing it away, she chose the latter since the chemical was too volatile to leave around the house. She went out back and dumped the remnant liquid down the privy.

Shortly thereafter, their grandfather had occasion to use the privy, sat down, pulled out his pipe, struck a match, lifted himself up on one ham and dropped the lit match down the glory hole. A tremendous explosion resulted and the old man was pitched quite a way into a pile of manure. Everybody came running, dug the old man out of his sanctuary and examined him carefully. Luckily no injuries had occured. "Grandpa! What happened? You had us scared to death."

"I dunno," the old man replied. "The only thing I kin figger is that it musta been somethin' I et."

———————————

They fed us so much pork that I grunted in my sleep and was plumb afraid to reach around and see if I had a curly tail.

———————————

The lady drove into a service station, poked her head out the window and asked the attendant if they had a rest room for ladies. He thought she said *whisk broom* and said,

"Ma'am, we don't have such around here but if you'll back to this here air hose, I'd be obliged to blow it out for ya."

The customer took off like a stung calf and the attendant watched her go, saying to himself, "I never could figure them women."

An Iowa farmer bought a used car but, after three days, he drove it back to the dealer's lot. "Anything wrong?" the dealer inquired warily.

"Nope," the farmer replied, grinning. "It's just that I thought it only fair to return these things to you 'cause they belong to that sweet old lady you told me was the owner of the car you sold me. Remember? She bought it new, only drove it to church on Sundays and treated it like her baby. Remember?

"Well, the poor dear left six cigars in the glove compartment, along with a box of condoms. And under the seat, I found this half-empty bottle of gin."

That feller is so danged crooked he has to screw on his socks.

A bicycle rider passed a farmhouse and noticed a little girl by the gate. She was sobbing and crying so pitifully that he braked and turned around to ask what was wrong. "Can't you hear 'em?" she sobbed.

"Oh!" the bicyclist said, alarmed, "What's going on with your parents?"

"They're up there yellin' and screamin' and I'm half scared to death."

"Whose little girl are you?"

"Well, that's what they're yellin' and screamin' and fightin' about."

The old gal hadn't lived no clean life. Fer shore, St. Pete won't consider her a candidate fer wings. Nope. She ain't goin' to be pickin' no grapes in the Lord's vineyard.

Old George decided he needed a bathroom added to his house. So he went to the bank to borrow five thousand dollars to do the job.

The banker had never previously loaned George money and was understandably cautious.

"Since this is the first time we've done business, George, would you mind telling me where you've done your business before?"

"Out back where we dug her out an' set her down in an oak thicket."

He was as full of gas as a runaway bull in a cornfield.

Down in Texas there is a chicken farmer who:
Had a Rhode Island hen that grew so tall
It took a whole dang month for the egg to fall.

My hired hand moved about as fast as a snail on a greased log. Why, he was so damn slow about doin' chores that no matter how hard he tried he couldn't stop quick. Once he laid down by the creek to git hisself a drink and the weeds grew over him.

Two farmers, neighbors, decided to take a day off and go hunting. They had trampled all morning and decided to rest at noon.

"You go fetch us some water, George," the older man said, "and I'll build us a fire and start lunch."

The younger farmer took off toward the river just past a nearby bull. Soon the young man appeared running back from the river.

"What's wrong, George?"

"There's the biggest damn water moccasin I ever saw down there. I just got the canteen filled, looked up and there, not three feet away, was a moccasin and that sucker must have been ten feet long!"

"Aw, you shouldn't a got so scared, George. Hell, that old

moccasin was a lot more scared of you than you of him."
   "Well, if that's so, this water ain't fit to drink."

He got beat bad. Lost enough hide to half-sole an elephant.

"When I left the ranch to go to college I was a three-letter man," said the cowboy.
   "I didn't know that they had athletic teams on your ranch."
   "They don't. I sat on a branding iron."

"We'll never have to retire and move to the city.
By the time we retire the city will be here."

He won't hurt ya. He's harmless as a bee in butter.

Chuck Jones was now an old man, but in his youth he had been one of the top cowboys in Texas. Now he sat on the fence, watching his grandson try to break a bronc. But each time his grandson mounted the horse, he got bucked off. After three failures, Chuck got impatient and yelled, "Hey, there, sonny, jest you git down off thet horse and let me show you how. It's been a long time, near twenty years, but I can still do her. Gimme a hand up and I'll show you."

Chuck got on the horse, with some help from his friends, and performed exactly as he had in his youth. He began to cuss the bronc. "Awright, now, you windblown , sagbacked, spavined son of a coyote, jist git goin' and do yore dangdest cause ya got a broncobuster on yo' now. Yippee!"

The bronc took a few still-legged steps, and then took off for the moon, came down hard, then fish-tailed and flew in the opposite direction. Old Chuck Jones took off for the sky and came down hard, picked himself up, slapped his leg with his Stetson, turned to his grandson and said: "Well, you saw how we did it in the old days. The trick is to know when the cayuse is ready to throw ya—then ya jump."

He's one heluva man. Got plenty fur on his brisket.

Back in 1890, they told the story of old Sam Jones who was known as the neighborhood chicken thief. He would swipe chickens right and left, but nobody ever caught him red-handed.

One morning old Sam noticed a note tacked to his cabin door. It read: "If you don't quit stealing my chickens, I'm going to skin you alive and then roast you for the buzzards."

Sam grabbed the note and rushed to the sheriff. "What am I supposed to do, Sheriff, this note scares the hell out 'n me."

"Well," said the sheriff, "to begin, you can stop stealin' chickens."

"How the hell can I do that," Sam replied, his teeth chattering, his hands shaking. "He didn't even sign his name!"

He angled over to the bar to git himself fortified against snake bite.

A farmer who enjoyed riding horses, saddled-up one Sunday afternoon and cantered off for a ride over his farm. When he approached the creek that ran along the boundary of his farm, he dismounted, tied his horse and sat down on the bank of the creek. He pulled out a pint of whiskey and proceeded to nip away at it. After about an hour, when the whiskey was almost finished, he noticed a rattlesnake slithering along the bank toward him. The snake stopped about three feet away and rattled furiously.

"Go ahead and strike, ya danged ol' rattler. I ain't never been more ready for ya!"

He sure is some dude. That ol' fancy Dan likes to set down at one of them fine resteraws that give ya thick tablecloths and thin soup.

Several farmers had been missing chickens from their poultry houses. They got together and everyone of them thought that one of their neighbors was guilty. Several poultry buyers had reported that the suspected neighbor seemed to be "steadily increasing" the size of his flock.

The farmers went to the sheriff and reported their suspicions. The sheriff got into his truck and drove to the suspected farm where he posed as a poultry buyer.

"These sure are nice birds," the sheriff remarked to the farmer.

"Yep. I feed 'em a special feed I invented. They get fatter and tastier than any chickens around here. Why, that feed is so tasty that the birds flock here from miles around . . . Rhode Island Reds, Leghorns, you name 'em. The chickens love my feed better than they love their home place." And the farmer winked elaborately at the sheriff.

"Is that so," remarked the poultry buyer. "You know who I am?"

"Yeah. You're the poultry buyer, ain't you?"

"Nope. I'm the sheriff."

"Well, do you know who I am?" asked the farmer, "I'm the biggest liar in this here country."

———————

You got as much chance of finding a thief in heaven as makin' lather outa laundry soap and alkali water.

———————

For many years Pete Brown had worked hard, saved his money and prayed to own a farm. After many frugal years, he found a farm he could afford. It was overgrown with brush and scrub trees and dotted with rocks and stumps. But Pete was an industrious worker and he fell to the job of cleaning the place, of making a farm out of it. And he succeeded!

Soon, after only a few years, Pete Brown had a decent farm with a bumper crop of soybeans, corn, wheat and clover.

One day the pastor came to visit him. "Brother Brown," the Pastor said, "There just is no doubt that you've done a bang-up job of reclaiming God's bit of earth. A wonderful job with God's green pasture."

"Yep. The Lord shure has been good to me. Sure has. But I want to tell you this, Pastor, it sure wasn't green like it is now when the Lord had it all to Himself."

———————

Them boots he had on was so fine you could see the wrinkles in his socks.

———————

Jones: There ain't nothin' lazier in the whole world than a blamed ol' mule.

Brown: Yes, there is. I got a rooster that's so lazy he waits for another rooster to crow . . . then he nods his head.

———————

He was a perpetual crap shooter, jest kept puttin' his money into circulation—over and over and over!

———————

During the depression an Ozarks farmer, Joshua Peters,

turned to illicitly making moonshine. And he did real well at it. He did so well that one of his neighbors grew jealous of his prosperity and reported him to a Federal agent who drove to the farm and put the moonshiner under arrest.

When it came time for the trial, they took old Joshua Peters out of his cell and placed him before the Federal Judge. The Judge, something of a bible student, studied the charges briefly and then, noting the man's name, said: "So, you're the Joshua who made the sun stand still?"

"Nope, Jedge. I ain't that one. I'm the one who made the moon shine."

It was so danged hot that if a feller died and went to hell he'd have to wire home for blankets.

A farmer whose family had been on the same farm for 100 years died. A huge crowd assembled to pay their respects to the deceased. The pastor preached an eloquent sermon, then turned to the assembled mourners and asked if any of them would like to say a few words in honor of the deceased.

He waited and waited, but nobody in the huge throng raised their hand or stood. It was embarrassing. Finally, an old time and perennial office holder stood and said: "If nobody has anything to add to the eloquent eulogy we've just heard, I'd like to say a few words about my candidacy for County Coroner."

He was so cockaloriously dressed-up that a full-feathered peacock hid his head in shame!

When the first farmers came to Sangamon County, Illinois, they cleared the ground and put in the family garden. This one farmer planted turnips and then pumpkins. As he left the field for dinner he noticed that the turnips were up and had good-sized fruit showing...already! But when he stopped to look at the turnips, the pumpkin vines almost caught him so that he ran for the fence (rail, of course) to escape. Alas, the vines caught him, held him fast so that to escape he reached for his knife. But he was too late. A big pumpkin had filled his pocket, growing fatter every second so that he couldn't get to his knife.

Fortunately, and just at this critical time, his wife came out of the house, saw the fix he was in, pulled up a turnip and, whirling it around by its leaves, hit that fat pumpkin in his pocket, and busted it to smitereens. Then she fished our the knife and cut her husband loose from the murderous vines.

They went back into the house, delighted that they had chosen rich ground to settle on. They told their descendants that it took only three of those turnips to fill a bushel basket and sometimes they had to cut one of those turnips in two—to make a dozen.

"I HATE static cling!"

With permission of *Country Magazine*

It was so hot the prunes was stewin' in their own juice.

"John!" the preacher exclaimed disapprovingly when, walking from church after the Sunday service, he spotted a member driving by on a tall load of hay. "Wouldn't it be better if you came to the service?"

"That's a good question, Parson. I don't know whether it's better to sit on a load of hay and think of God—or sit in church and think of hay."

———————————

We warned him. And shore enough, he ended up climbin' the golden stairs at the end of a rope.

———————————

Out in Texas they tell the story of this calm and reasonable rancher who, one day, was trying to persuade a cow to get in the trailer. Using the most reasonable, endearing terms, he tried and tried but the cow was not reassured. Actually, she pinned the old boy against the fence.

But sweet words seemed to work because the old cow backed off and let the rancher loose. He told her it was always better to be peaceable and considerate and that she should think things over quietly while he went outside the corral for a few moments.

He returned with a six foot post, smiled at her gently, then suggested that she go sweetly into the trailer. But the old girl seemed not to have learned a thing. She charged the rancher who then hit her over the head, knocked her to her knees and said, "Now git the hell up off yore knees and git in that thar truck."

She got.

Which just goes to show that on the ranch or farm, a fellow can catch more flies with sugar but a heavy post is a heluva lot better when it comes to loading cows.

———————————

My horse throwed me fork-end up.

———————————

The harvest of wheat is a chore;
I itch, and I'm tired and sore.
But the city's pollution
Presents no solution—
So I'll just go combine some more!

Mrs. Jerry Hamilton of Centerville, Indiana

It's hotter than the hind hubs of hell!

On our farm we raise Herefords, it's true,
But Hereford's our family name, too.
So when folks see our small herd
Then ask, "How're the Herefords?"
We reply, "They're just fine—
we are, too!"

Koneda L. Hereford of Southside, West Virginia

Ain't nothin' hurts like when a horse grasses ya.

Amos and a half a dozen old neighbors, all retired farmers, were sitting around the stove in the village store, discussing the mysteries of existence and swapping tales of the aches and pains of growing old.

"I'm going deaf and blind," Amos complained. "I don't know what the Good Lord wants to leave me here for."

"Now, Amos," one of his friends protested, "The Lord's ways are not our ways. We can't always understand them. But if he's left you here it's because he's got work for you to do."

Amos pondered this statement briefly, then declared himself: "Well, I ain't agonna do it!"

His head was empty as a posthole that ain't been filled up.

Two youngsters were bragging about the quality of poultry on their fathers' farm: "Our hens are real doers," the one boy said. "Why, last winter we had a hen that sat on a piece of ice and hatched out two quarts of hot water and a cup of tea."

"That's nothing," the other kid said. "Last year we ran out of feed and Paw fed the old hen sawdust. And do you know that hen hatched out chicks with one wooden leg and there were two woodpeckers."

It was so hot you could fry eggs on the sidewalks.

There was a young man from the city
Who thought that our daughter was pretty.
But when hay was all baled
His poor back had derailed—
And his asthma attack was a pity!

This winsome young lad was no quitter;
Janie's smile had his heart all a-twitter.
He bragged cows he'd soon master,
Then learned bulls can run faster—
Almost went back to town in a litter!

This fellow at last said, "Enough!
This life on the farm's just too rough.
It's loaded with danger,
But what's even stranger—
To these country folks . . . it ain't tough!"

Jeanette Wodarski, Dundee

He had that turrible disease called bottle fever.

They tell of a farmer south of Columbia, Missouri who wished to hire a hand. A young fellow came and applied for the job. "Well, I'll tell you," said the farmer, "I want a man who never gets hungry and never gets tired." "I'm the one you want," answered the young man. And so he was hired.

About the middle of the forenoon, the farmer saw the young hand stop work and go to the house. When the farmer went to the house to investigate, there sat the hand eating.

"I thought you never got hungry nor tired," said the irate farmer.

"Why, I don't. I eat before I get hungry and rest before I get tired," calmy replied the new hand.

The farmer kept him for four years.

Thet boy would eat anything that wasn't moving.

On a suburban farm adjacent to the high school football

field, a rooster noticed that a football had landed in the poultry run. He called all the hens to him and cackled, "I'm not grumbling ladies, not complaining at all. But I merely want you to see for yourselves what the girls are doing in other places."

Did you hear about the simple farmer who used a toothbrush on the cow's teeth? Now she's giving . . . you won't believe this . . . dental cream.

See ya next week, if God's willin' and the creek don't rise.

There was this indecisive farmer who couldn't decide that which he wanted more . . . a new cow or a bicycle. "You'll look mighty silly riding around the farm on a cow," his wife said.
"Yeah, but I'd look sillier milking a bicycle!"

Y'all come on back, y'hear, when ya cain't stay so long!

A farmer was queried on the primary use of cowhide. His reply was just right, appropriate to the silliness of the question.
"My paw always told me that the main use of the hide of a cow was to hold the cow together."

Here's hopin' you'll be in heaven an hour before the devil knows you're dead.

A lot of people criticize the folks who love to raise horses. But there's one thing you can say about horses . . . you don't have to fill 'em with alcohol to keep 'em from freezing.

It's colder than a cast-iron seat in a tin privy on the shady side of an iceberg.

The banker was talking very learnedly about money and banking.

"Assets," he said, "Do you know what assets are?"

"Sure. Every rancher knows that," was the reply. "They are little donkeys."

Well, if that don't tear the plank off the house!

The farmer had purchased a mule at a war surplus sale. The mule had the customary U.S. stamped on his hindquarters. "I see that your new mule has U.S. stamped on his rump," the farmer's neighbor said. "Does that mean he was a U.S. mule?"

"Nope, that doesn't stand for Uncle Sam. Nosiree. That stands for 'Unsafe'."

I ain't gonna ride through that brush. No siree! Why I'd need me a outfit made by a blacksmith.

A prim young lady asked a rancher about the severe kick he'd received from a mule. "Just where did he kick you?"

The rancher, diplomatic and modest, replied: "Well, if my head was in New York and my feet in California, he'd have kicked me right smack in . . . in . . . Omaha."

For many years this Iowa farmer had done nothing but complain. It was either too wet or too dry, prices were too low or his check too slow in coming. He was never satisfied. Then, one day, he came to town after a particularly good year. Temperatures, weather, prices, all were of record proportions—especially the yields. A friend asked him about the year and he replied, looking terribly down-hearted: "It was the best crop I ever raised."

"Then why are you looking so glum? You ought to be dancing in the streets."

"That's what you think! Why, man it's terrible to think about the tons and tons of fertility, the nitrogen, phosphates, calcium and lots more that there big crop took out of the soil."

He's so danged stingy he crawls under the gates to keep the hinges from wearin' out.

Two country kids were visiting their grandparents in town. They wandered around and ended up at the new school where electricians were putting on the finishing touches.

"What are you doing?" the one kid asked.

"We're just finishing up the electrical work, putting in electrical switches," replied one of the workers.

"Boy oh boy!" exclaimed one of the kids. "I'm sure glad that we still got our old country school."

That kid is bright as a head of cabbage in a pumpkin field.

In Maine there is a farmer who is most cautious about what he says. One day this farmer was approached by a stranger who asked him about his superb Angus bull; "How much is that dandy bull of yours worth?"

The farmer hesitated, considering, then replied, "Are you the tax assessor or has he been hit by a truck?"

That feller was as welcome as forty miles of bad road.

A farmer had suffered from drought for several years. But a good-hearted storekeeper in the nearby town had carried him on the books during all the bad times. Then came change with bumper crops and great prices for cattle and hogs. The farmer paid his debt to the storekeeper but then didn't return to do business for over a year.

The storekeeper met the farmer together with his three sons and noticed they were driving an expensive new car and all were wearing expensive new suits. "How is it," the storekeeper asked, "that when I carried you on my books for so many years you traded with me. But now that you're doing good you go shop someplace else?"

The farmer seemed shocked, then almost cried. "Dammit all, anyway," he groaned. "I didn't realize you sold for cash."

He's so dumb he don't know straight up from applesauce.

"How are things going on the farm?"

"Not so hot. Things are so bad I can't pay the hired man his wages. So he works until he's got enough money to buy the farm, then I work for him until he owes me enough money to buy the farm back. That's how we get along."

That feller's workin' without a full string of lights.

They tell the story about the city fellow who bought a farm. It had two windmills. But after his first year on the farm, the city man took down one of them.

"Why did you take it down?" his neighbor asked.

"I ran short of water," was the reply. "And I figured it was the lack of wind. So, not having enough for two windmills, I took the one down."

"Did that solve your water problem," the neighbor asked, grinning.

"Not yet."

If brains was leather thet feller wouldn't have enough to saddle a fly.

A farmer was complaining to his city cousin that life on the farm was not easy. "We go to sleep with the chickens, get up with the roosters, work like a horse, eat like a pig and then get treated like a dog."

Sometimes I feel about farming something like the one-legged man at a kickin' contest—about that much chance!

This busy farmer had no time to plant a family garden. So, when his wife needed a cabbage for dinner, she asked him to go to town and get one. "What size?" he asked.

"About . . . about . . . oh, pick one about the size of your head," she replied.

So he left. On the way he met a friend who invited him to go into his garden and pick a head of cabbage. "Take any head you want," he said.

After the friend had gone into the house, his wife said, "That is some dumb jerk in our garden. Why, he's been out there half an hour trying his hat on one cabbage after another."

If you yelled in his ears he'd hear only an echo.

Talk about passionate girlfriends! This one farmer told his friend:

"Why, that l'il old gal is so hot she held an egg in each hand and hatched four chicks."

His neighbor said, "You call that hot? Why, I know a gal who put her hand on a corn stalk and the entire 40 acres caught fire. The cops took her in for arson. You know what? The iron bars in her cell melted and she climbed out scot-free."

The crackers in bed didn't bother him at all. But the crumb in the closet did!

Johnny was visiting his uncle's farm for the first time. He was helping him put up hay in a huge stack near the barn, working on top spreading the hay pitched up to him. When they were finished he called down, "Hey, Uncle George, how am I going to get down?"

Uncle George studied the problem for a time, then yelled

up: "Oh, just shet yer eyes and walk around a bit."

Dumb! That feller couldn't track an elephant in three feet of snow.

At last the farmer finished his big cattle barn. He was very busy in the field and told his new hired hand to cut a hole beside the door so that the cat could get out or in.

The new hand cut the opening beside the barn door. When the farmer inspected the work he was furious. "How come," he yelled, "you put the hole alongside the barn door? That's the dumbest thing that's happened in twenty years."

"Why?" asked the hired hand.

"Because, you dummy, when you swing the door open, well, then where is your derned hole? Covered, that's where. And then how do you expect the cat to get out!"

That ol' feller is six cookies short of a dozen!

A horse breeder was discussing veterinary problems with another breeder. "I sent a letter off to the vet school and asked them what I should do to cure my horse of the slobbers."

"Yeah? What did they tell you?"

"The dern fools wrote back that I should teach him to spit."

There's no reason for those guys to be veterinarians! Why? They don't send donkeys to school 'cause nobody likes a smart ass, that's why!

"What in the world is that gruesome smell out here?" the city girl asked the farmer.

"That's fertilizer."

"Well, for the land's sake!" exclaimed the city girl.

"Yep," said the farmer.

That man'll do to ride the river with. You bet! He measures a full sixty hands high and he's square as a quarter section.

"But you SAID you wanted a double garage!"

With permission of *Country Magazine*

A keen and curious young Boston woman, paying her first visit to a farm, was being shown about the place by the friendly owner.

"Why is it that some of your cows have horns and some have none?" the young woman asked.

"Well," said the farmer, "there are three cases in which cows may lack horns: Some are born without them, some have been dehorned and some have had their horns knocked off while fighting."

"I see," the woman said with interest. "Now, what about that different one over there in the corner of the field?"

"That's case No. 4," the farmer said. "That's a horse."

That li'l old gal was about as popular as a turd in chicken soup.

John Gibbons could handle the toughest animals, lift the

biggest loads and get more work done than any farmer in the neighborhood.

But when he was past 60, he was seized with a searing pain. It was his appendix, and he reluctantly agreed to enter the hospital.

Still, the doctors and nurses found John to be a difficult patient. He didn't see any sense in much of anything they wanted him to do. Finally, though, they managed to wheel him into the operating room for surgery.

The next morning, when the doctor looked in on John, he found him sitting in a chair, smoking his pipe, dressed and straining to pull on his heavy boots.

"Hey!" the doctor yelled. "You shouldn't be sitting up yet. You'll tear your stitches out!"

John stared back angrily at the doctor. "What's the matter, Doc?" he muttered. "Ain't your thread no good?"

That ol' feller measures a full sixteen hands high. He's got plenty sand and is plumb full of fightin' tallow.

"Grandpa," the young farm boy asked. "were boys better behaved in your day than they are now?"

"They sure were," Grandpa responded. "Back then, when we saw a young fellow beginnin' to sow his wild oats . . . we started up the thrashin' machine!"

A South Dakota cowboy was in Mexico for the first time, and naturally he had to go see a bullfight.

For a while, he watched impatiently as the matador repeatedly waved his red cape in front of the bull and then gracefully stepped aside when the animal charged. The action looked like nonsense to the cowboy, who finally yelled out:

"Hey, Mister! You ain't never goin' to catch that critter unless you hold your sack still!"

Never interfere with nothin' that don't bother you.

Who says that I'm old and over the hill?
Who says what I could do I can't do still?
Who says, though I work just as hard as I can,
I can't keep up with a much younger man?
Who says, though I'll still glance at a lassie,
I don't take as long a-viewing the chassis?
Who says I can't work hard all the day long,
And then, at midnight, still be going strong?
Who says these things and swears they are true?
I'll tell you who says them . . . by golly, I do!

Wayne E. Eicher, Napoleon, Ohio

He looks as though one more clean shirt would be just enough.

Why is it

. . . your highest-producing cow always steps on her teat?

. . . your nose always itches when your hands are covered with manure?

. . . on a night you're rushing to get done early, the cows refuse to come in from the pasture?

. . . every time you open your mouth in the dairy barn, a cow puts her tail in it?

"I ain't afraid o' water. In fact I like a little of it for a chaser once in a while."

There was an old lady in Brewster,
Annoyed by an awfully mean rooster.
She said, "Quit your crowing
Or in the pot you'll be going!"
Now the rooster don't crow like he used-ter!

Thet old rooster was as useless as a pump without a handle.

How to Preserve a Husband

Some wives insist on keeping their husband in a pickle, while others keep them in hot water. This only makes them sour, hard and bitter. Even poor varieties may be made sweet, tender and good by garnishing them with patience, well-sweetened with smiles and flavored with kisses to taste. Then wrap them in a mantle of charity, keep warm with a steady fire of domestic devotion and serve with peaches and cream.

When thus prepared, husbands will keep for years!

Good Neighbor Recipe

1 tongue that does not slander
1 mind full of tolerance
2 ears closed to gossip
2 eyes overlooking others' faults
1 heart generous and kind
2 hands extended to help others
1 dash wit, smiles and sunny disposition

Blend together the above ingredients. Form into one being. Serve generous portions to everyone you meet!

Mrs. Ben L. Yoder, Jr., Riverside, Iowa

That woman was top of the heap. With her love was an itch she couldn't scratch.

Donita Flatt of Engadine, Michigan says her neighbors placed this classified ad in their local newspaper when they put their Shetland ponies up for sale:

"FOR SALE: 1976 Shetland Ponies, 4-on-the-floor, single exhaust, approx. 40 miles to the bale @ $75. Nice Compact."

It's clear enough . . . that li'l ol' horse is a doozie.

There was a farm wife name of Bell
Who slipped and fell into the well.
When she started to shout
Her false teeth fell right out—
What she said next is not fit to tell!

Mrs. James Cotton, Creston, Ohio

When President Roosevelt took over the Depression from Herbert Hoover, he sent fellows all over the country, plowing up cotton, drowning little pigs, etc. So one of these young fellows came down to southern Illinois from Washington, D.C. to kill and bury some of the excess animals. But being a city feller, he knew little about farm stock.

Well, he found an old billy goat about to starve to death on a run-down farm. So he called back to Washington and reported, "Say, there's a funny animal down here, long and skinny. He's wearing a long beard and smells terrible. What are my orders?" Immediately the word came back, "For heaven's sake, don't kill it. That's a southern Illinois farmer."

He's so dumb he couldn't pour piss out of a boot with instructions in capital letters on the heel.

Two hard-working but far-from-rich farmers were taking a break one day when the talk turned to money.

"Just supposin' you made a million dollars one year from farming," one said to the other. "What would you do with it?"

The second farmer slowly tamped down his pipe, then answered, "I reckon I'd leave every last cent of it to my heirs."

"What?" the first farmer exclaimed. "You mean to tell me you wouldn't even spend a nickel on yourself?"

"I don't reckon I'd have the time," the second farmer explained. "I figger I'd already be dead from the shock."

You are a squirrel's idea of the Promised Land. You're nuts.

_____

The self-confident old farmer on the witness stand was a troublesome customer for the brash young district attorney.

"Are you acquainted with any of the gentlemen on this jury?" the young fellow inquired.

"More than half, I'd say," the farmer replied.

"Well," the district attorney pressed on, "Are you willing to _swear_ that you know more than half of them?"

The old man looked slowly over the panel of 12 men, good and true.

"If it comes to that," he finally drawled, "I'm willing to swear I know more'n all of 'em put together!"

_____

All asses do not travel on four feet.

_____

When they travel on business, farmers are not likely to throw money around carelessly . . . since they have to approve and pay their own expense accounts.

After 500 farmers had attended a convention in Chicago, a hotel man there shook his head and reported, "Each one of them came here with a $10 bill in one pocket and the Ten Commandments in the other—and left town without breaking either one!"

_____

You can make about as much money off a farmer as you can shearin' a pig.

_____

Snooze Alarm

Working hours in agriculture are usually a bit longer than the usual 8-to-5 city routine . . . on occasion, quite a bit longer. Western South Dakotans tell this tale:

A cowhand, riding his horse from one ranch to a new job 50 miles away, stopped at a ranch and asked for overnight hospitality. In the usual fashion, he was invited to eat and spend the night.

Next morning his hosts were loading cattle for the long haul to market, and they rose extra early to get the work under way before the day grew too hot. Because of this, the cowhand—who knew nothing of the plans for the day—was called to breakfast at 3 a.m.

"Holy mackerel!" the surprised cowhand grumbled. "It sure don't take long to stay all night at this place!"

Ain't he a sniggle fritz!

Should've Chicked First!

"Dear Sir," a poultry dealer wrote to a farmer. "That crate you shipped those hens in was so dilapidated it fell apart while I was bringing it out from the depot. All the hens got away, and I only rounded up 10 of them. Here's my check for those 10."

The dealer received a prompt reply, "Congratulations on your vigilance," the farmer wrote. "I'll certainly be glad to deal with you again—there were only eight hens in that crate when it left here."

He's so stupid he thought manual labor was a chicano.

———————

On special occasions and under particular circumstances, farmers have been known to exaggerate the truth slightly.

"Terrible dry summer," one farmer complained. "Never did see the grass grow as short as mine did."

"You think *yours* was short," a second farmer hooted. "I had to lather mine before I could use the mowing machine!"

———————

It's hotter than honeymoon sheets.

———————

"Dad lives, as he has for 80 years, in the mountainous region of northern Idaho. Out there, there are but two directions—uphill and downhill!

"Anyway, Dad recently came to visit me in my little hideaway on the 'back-side of the desert'. He scanned my land silently for a few minutes, then remarked, 'You folks around here waste too much ground. Where I come from, we stand it up on end—and farm three sides of it!' "

Bonnie Morgan of Zillah, Washington

———————

That old feller is entitled to a warm corner

———————

A Kansas farmer had built a fine, modern house. After carpets and draperies were installed, his wife decided one of the walls needed a nice painting, preferably a colorful oil.

"You have to go to Kansas City next week with cattle anyway," the farm wife told her husband. "Why not hunt around and find one there?"

The next week, the farmer returned home from his trip with a painting. After it had been hung, his wife stepped back to survey the effect.

The painting was definitely of the abstract school—a mass of daubs and streaks in many shades and colors but with absolutely no discernible pattern. "Darling," the farm wife said, "it's exactly right for that wall. But I'm surprised you picked an abstract—what in the world does that painting mean?"

"Honey," the farmer replied, "that's no abstract. The way I see it, it's a perfect representation of the farm situation—any way you hang it and any way you look at it, it doesn't make sense!"

———————

Thet kinda looks like a Christmas ornament hung on an oak tree.

———————

I envy my friend in the city,
Where the lawns and walks are clean,
And there when her guests are greeted,
The hostess is calm and serene.
But woe is me in the country,
My guests are prepared for the worst;
It makes no difference where they walk—
My chickens have been there first.

Dorothy Knouse-Koepke, Hoskins, Nebraska

———————

Great gobs of gallopin' goosegrease.

———————

There once was a man with a Deere
Who couldn't quite get it in gear.
But what's even worse
When he DID hit reverse
He flew to the next hemisphere!

M.L. Gerber of West Bend, Iowa

———————

That feller humped his tail at the short end and lit a shuck fer somewhere.

———————

Businessman Ralph Jones left his executive office behind on earth and headed for the Pearly Gates.

When he announced himself to St. Peter, that bearded old angel scratched his head and consulted his list. "Well, Mr. Jones," St. Peter said with a bit of surprise in his voice, "your name *is* on my list..."

Jones passed through the Gates and was immediately surrounded by several other former businessmen. "Look!" they chorused, "old Ralph made it after all. Let's celebrate!"

Next in line at the Pearly Gates was a man with callused hands, dressed in overalls and wearing work boots, St. Peter asked his name and occupation.

"I'm Sam Brown," the man said. "I was a farmer."

St. Peter nodded. "Go right in," he said without consulting his list.

Brown passed through the Gates and looked around. "Isn't there going to be any celebration for me?" he asked.

"Naw," St. Peter replied. "There're so many of you farmers up here, we can't throw a party for every new one that shows up."

Them farm boys is straight as a wagon tongue, up and down as a cow's tail, and stand high above their corns.

Said a farmer, "It's really a sin;
I'm in the worse fix that I've been.
These hogs I'm not grazing
On the corn I'm not raising
Are becoming exceedingly thin!"

Louise Merchant of Huntsville, Arkansas

If brains were ink, you'd never dot an "i."

Lillian F. Ward of Laverne, Oklahoma passes this little chuckle along:

A rich farmer was on his deathbed. He told his wife to take his billfold up on the roof of the farmhouse and put it under a shingle, so when he went to Heaven he could pick it up as he went by.

A few days after his death, his wife went up to the roof and looked under the shingle. Sure enough, the billfold was still there.

"Just as I thought," clucked his wife. "He's gone to the *other* place."

Her cookies ain't fully baked.

Anne Coleman of Rapidan, Virginia relates this cute kid's quote from the mouth of her daughter's godson:

"The boy, who was 3, and his mother had just returned home from a weeklong visit to Grandma and Grandpa's farm," Anne says.

"The mother was very proud of all the farming knowledge her little boy had acquired during the visit, so she asked him, 'David, what do we get from cows?'

"David's reply? 'Messy feet'!"

That kid's as welcome as water in your boot!

A farmhand was handed a pay envelope which, by mistake, contained a blank check.

He looked at it and moaned, "Just what I thought would happen—my deductions finally caught up with my salary."

My boss has short arms and long pockets.

A Wyoming rancher was suddenly stricken with severe chest pains. He went to the physician specializing in diseases of the chest. This physician was not familiar with ranch life . . . especially this particular rancher's life. He prescribed as follows:

"I do believe that you, sir, are lacking in fresh air. Could you arrange to sleep in the open air for a few weeks?"

"Well, I could try," the rancher replied. "I been sleepin' under the chuck wagon most nights but I reckon I could kick a couple of spokes out'n of the wheels."

It's so cold my drawers feel like they're made of fish net.

While in town, ordering supplies for her farmer husband, the dealer congratulated her on her knowledge of agriculture. "You must have grown up on the farm," he said.

"No, I didn't," the woman replied. "Actually, I grew up in the city. As a matter of fact, until I met my husband, I had never seen a pig."

"The game of love is dug with little digs."

There was a sweet calf on our farm
Who we thought could never do harm.
But things have changed now;
She's an onery old cow—
And the cause of this cast on my arm!

Sue Skifton of Caledonia, Minnesota

That critter was techy as a teased snake.

Rather proud of the son who was leaving for his senior year at the college where he had done well, a farmer decided they ought to have their picture taken together.

The photographer suggested the boy stand with his hand on his father's shoulder, but the farmer disagreed.

"It would look more natural" he said, "if you'd have him stand with his hand in my pocket."

A small town is where almost nobody can get away with

lying about the year they were born. Too many people remember.

___

In town for a few hours while waiting to meet his boss, a cowboy wandered into the blacksmith's shop. He picked up a horseshoe, not knowing it had just come from the forge. Instantly he dropped the shoe, shoved his seared hand into his pocket and tried to look nonchalant.

"Kinda hot, wasn't it?" the blacksmith asked.

"Nope," the cowboy replied. "Just don't take me long to look at a horseshoe."

___

Thet ol' boy ain't got enuff brains to pound sand down a prairie dog hole.

___

Three dogs were out together. One belonged to a preacher, one to a gambler and one to a farmer. The three dogs got lost in the woods.

Said the preacher's dog, "I'm going to pray, and God will show me the way out."

Declared the gambler's dog, "I'm going to take a chance on finding my own way out."

"Not me," said the farmer's dog. "I'm going to sit and wait. There'll be a government man along soon!"

___

Holy smokes, fiddlesticks, and great jumpin' Jehoshuphat!

___

Mrs. Jack Luethi of Independence, Wisconsin, says she recently spotted this sign on a farmhouse lawn near her place:

"For Sale—one set of encyclopedias. Never used—teenage son knows everything."

___

What can you expect from a kid of fryin' size!

___

"Why," asked the irritated farmer of his hired hand, "did it take you so long to get home from town with those mules?"

"Sorry," explained the hand, "but I picked up Reverend Davis on the way home—and from then on those mules couldn't understand a word I said."

It's enough to make a preacher lay his Bible down.

A traveling salesman was going to a new prospect, taking shortcuts through the back country, when he passed what seemed a mirage, so totally out-of-place was this elaborate farm with many beautiful barns and a mansion.

As he passed a neat fence he noticed a pig inside it that had a wooden leg. So surprised was the salesman that he stopped the car and took a second look. "This is too much," he thought, turned around and went back to the mansion, stopped the car, got out and went up to the house. The farmer met him at the door.

"Howdy, stranger. What can I do for you?" the farmer asked.

"I'm real curious to know about the pig out there, the one with the wooden leg. How come?"

"Socrates? Oh, you're talking about Socrates. He's the best hog a man could ever hope to have. Plumb genius. Why, that old hog has done me more good than throwing twenty consecutive sevens, shooting craps. Yessir.

"See that oil rigging over there? Well, old Socrates snuffed the place out for the prospectors, showed 'em exactly where to drill and the oil out of that well pays me ninety thousand a year.

"Then looky over yonder. See that mine shaft and outbuildings? Well, Socrates snuffed out the place and now I get about two hundred thousand a year—just for me—out of it. Royalty or some such thing, they call it.

"Then, one night about two years ago a robber came to the house took all my money and was about to shoot me when old Socrates busted in, grabbed the bum by the leg and liked to of tore the damned leg off him. Saved my life. . . ."

"Well that sure is some hog," the salesman said. "But

you still haven't told me why he's got a wooden leg."

"Oh yes, I plumb forgot. The wooden leg.... Well, you know how it is. Gratitude plays a big part in it. When you own a hog that does all that much for you, you sure as hell don't eat him all at one time."

———————

If bullshit was music you'd have one heluva brass band.

———————

... to the Other

A traveller from the wet delta region of Arkansas, attracted by the reports of a land where rain was a novelty, decided to go to the Southwest for relief. When asked why, he replied:

"This dang Delty's too wet for ME. Why, here the onliest time the sun EVER shines is when it rains. Even the pores uv ma hide air sproutin' WATER CRESS. But I could stand ma ole houn'dawg havin' crawdads 'stid uv fleas; fer water bugs to take the place uv flies; fer the chickens to grow web footed an' their aigs to hatch out turtles. Why I just laffed at the bullfrogs croakin' on the haid uv ma bed; at the pollywogs in the drinkin' water; an' I even stood it without too much cussin' when all the young'uns took down with water rash an' the ole woman got water-on-th-knee. But, when I started ketchin' CATFISH in the settin' room MOUSE TRAP, I figgered 'twuz time to MOVE!"

"Awright!
Who hasn't had their teeth clipped?"

With permission of *Country Magazine*

Thiseyer wet weather gits plumb wholesale.

The Dirt Farmer
by Abe Martin

In spite o' th' Turkish question an' King Tut's tomb, th' fate o' th' farmer continues t' be discussed.

What's t' be done fer th' farmer, what's t' become o' th' farmer, how's he gittin' on, an' what he's thinkin' t' himself are bein' liberally talked about by statesmen, businessmen an' loafers.

Lots o' big questions bob up an' die out, but it's purty hard t' start a conversation about anything without finally gittin' down t' th' farmer.

Th' administration at Washin'ton seems t' really seriously want t' do somethin' fer th' farmer, but it don't seem t' be able t' do anything fer anybuddy, not even itself.

Once in a while it appoints a "dirt farmer" t' somethin', but it's allus some feller that wouldn' know a double tree from a pair o' wooden hames—most likely some feller that rents out his wife's farm an' lives in town an' dabbles in politics.

Tornado Insurance Agent Tell Binkley has held two gover'ment jobs—one as a representative o' labor, an' one as a "dirt farmer."

Lem Small, our "dirt farmer" sheriff, travelled fer a dry goods house fer th' past thirty years. Years an' years ago he weaned a calf an' has been t' law twice over a line fence, but he's never put in a crop, or tried t' make money on milk.

When an administration wants t' appoint a banker or a political fixer it never gits confused an' appoints a farmer.

The best year around temperature is a warm heart and a cool head.

Just a line to say I'm living,
That I'm not among the dead,
Though I'm getting more forgetful
And more mixed-up in my head.

For sometimes I can't remember
When at the foot of the stairs
If I'm going up for something
Or just came down from there.

And before the 'fridge so often
My poor mind is full of doubt:
Have I come to put the food away
Or come to take it out?

And there's times when it's dark outside
With my nightcap on my head
I don't know if I'm retiring
Or getting out of bed.

So if it's my time to write you
There's no need for getting sore,
I may think that I have written
And don't want to be a bore.

So remember I do love you
And I wish that you were here,
But now it's nearly mail time so
I must say good-bye, my dear.

Now I stand beside the mailbox
With my face a crimson red;
Though I meant to mail my letter
I have opened it instead!

Royce C. Holloway of Albany, Oregon

He don't travel like a colt no more.

ENOS had just celebrated his 99th birthday, and a young newspaper reporter visited Enos at his farm to do an interview about his longevity.

As the reporter left, he told Enos, "I hope I can come back next year and congratulate you on your 100th birthday!"

"Don't know why you couldn't," Enos answered politely. "You look healthy enough to me."

That old man's got plenty of wrinkles on his horns.

A farmer in Kansas had such a reputation for stinginess that the Federal Wage and Hour Administration sent an operative to investigate his tactics.

"I've been told," the operative said to the farmer, "that you are violating the law by paying below the minimum wage."

"You have, eh?" the farmer retorted. "Well, let's see."

"There's Jake, who milks the cows and listens to the radio most of the day. He gets $40 a week. Then there's Hanneb, who's supposed to do the cooking but reads love stories and fan magazines most of the time. She gets $35. And there's my son, Cal, who kicks footballs through the windows and drives off in the car every night. He gets $30."

"Nothing wrong with that," admitted the government man. "Anybody else to tell about?"

"Just the half-wit," mused the farmer. "He works 18 hours a day and gets $10 a week."

"What!" said the operative. "Well, I'd like to speak to him."

"You are," said the farmer.

Helen Palmer of Ithaca, Michigan

That's so funny it'd make a stuffed bird laugh.

Farmers are the most proficient lawyers in the world. They don't specialize in criminal law, or corporate law, or even tax law—their domain is *Murphy's Law*.

Who's Murphy? Well, he must have been a farmer, for he developed the premise "What can go wrong, will go wrong."

Murphy's Law is the backbone of agriculture . . . no farmer could practice without it. Consider the evidence . . .

The engine and the warranty always expire together.

The bean market rises 20¢ on the day after you sell.

Interchangeable . . . won't.

Unbreakable . . . isn't.

Smartweed . . . is.

"Guaranteed" means "Good Luck."

You end up with 11 rows left to plant with a 12-row planter.

Nails only puncture the inside dual.

Cutworms dine on insecticide.

Cockleburrs only grow in the row.

Implement dealers always lack just *one* part. Yours.

"Improved" means a new package. And a higher price.

The markets are good when you have nothing to sell.

The wrong part comes in the right box.

That feller was bred in Missouri but he's sure a crumb here!

"Field-ready" is . . . after 3 days of tightening bolts.

The radiator eats a hole at 5:05 p.m. Friday. And Stop Leak doesn't.

"Labor-saving" means at the factory.

A 10% chance of rain brings 2 inches.

New overshoes leak on the first day out of the box.

The right tool is never in the chest.

You have every size bolt . . . except the one you need.

The combine breaks down the last day of harvest.

"Reworked" means "repainted."

The cab air conditioner breaks down in July; the heater, in December.

It always rains the day you load hogs.

The auger breaks at the top of the bin.

You have three left gloves. And no right ones.

"Never grease" means "soon will cease."

The weather is either too hot, too cold, too dry, too wet—or too good to last.

A farmer always thinks next year will be better.

Connie Klug of Stockport, Iowa

Farmin' can make you nervous as a fly in a can of glue.

Allurin' Facts About Floridy
by Abe Martin

Clint Peabody, who stole a set o' harness here in th' early days before th' auto, is in town smokin' cigars an' lookin' like a delegate t' a haberdasher's conclave.

Clint's been farmin' in Floridy, but last week he sold his farm fer $285,000, an' a $5,000,000 hotel is t' stand where he used to git discouraged.

"But farmin', next t' th' hotel business, is th' great comin' industry in Floridy.

"Anything'll grow in Floridy that'll grow in Ceylon," says Clint.

"While you folks used t' be standin' in snow up t' your pants pockets in front o' th' pust office, I wuz pickin' cumquats.

"But Christmus is th' funniest thing in Floridy. You can't give mufflers an' gloves, an' sleds. You've got t' think up somethin' else.

"I gave my wife two bolts o' mosquito bar, an' a red ant sprayer last Christmus as she already had some white stockin's.

"Floridy raises more celery than Montana an' Nevada combined, while her p'tater crop is greater than those o' New Mexico an' Louisville, Kentucky, put t'gether.

"An' next t' Californy, her orange crop beats any state in th' Union.

"An' we have alligators which no other state has.

"Our green corn an' beans, an' t'maters reach th' New York market jest about th' time you're tryin' t' thaw out your kitchen pumps.

"You kin eat our strawberries on New Year's day if you've got th' price.

"All th' time you folks are huddled around th' settin' room stove, dreadin' feedin' time, an' tryin' t' coax one another t' go down t' th' letter box an' git th' mail, I'm shippin' pineapples t' th' Northern market an' gittin' ready t' loaf all summer.

"One o' th' beauties o' Floridy is that you kin milk in th' open th' year around, an' you have no best overcoat that's turned red on th' shoulders t' worry about.

"An' th' fishin'! You don't have t' fish. You jest go down t' th' ocean an' they give 'emselves up.

"Floridy is goin' t' be some state in a few months.

"Already ther's enough lots platted at Sarasoty alone t' make a city of 100,000,000.

"No other state in th' Union offers th' facilities fer loafin' that Floridy does.

"Ther's more Northerners in Miamy that never expect t' work agin than ther is in all th' rest o' the country put t'gether.

"A feller that haint too proud t' wear blue denim an' who likes cocoanuts kin live cheaper in Floridy than he kin with his wife's folks."

———

Let's pray that the wind at your back may never be your own.

———

Two old men were discussing world problems and had come to the subject of overpopulation.

"Sure is awful, all them kids they're abreedin' these days. Why, they say that by the year 2000 there ain't gonna be nothin' but standin room only."

"That so?" replied the other old fellow. He nodded his head sagely and said, "Well, that ought to slow 'em down a little."

———

"Her baby is a direct descendant of the long line she listened to and believed!

———

The farm lad left the home place, went to Chicago and became a bus driver. Just off Monroe Street, a fellow with a Saint Bernard tried to get on his bus. "You can't get on this bus with that dog, mister," said the ex-farm boy.

"Why not?" snapped the fellow.

"No dogs allowed, that's why."

"O.K. And you know what you can do with your Goddam bus!"

"Listen, buddy," the driver retorted. "You do the same with your hound and I'll let you on!"

That man is so nasty that when he looks in the mirror, his image throws up.

New England farmers are the most individualistic of them all. And Vermont breeds the most stubborn of all. They tell about this retired farmer who was advised, by his physician, to install a telephone in his room. He did.

One day a friend was visiting him when the phone rang. And it rang again and again. "Why don't you answer the damned thing, man. It's your telephone. Did you forget?"

"Nope. Didn't fergit," responded the old boy. "But I put that phone in for *my* convenience and nobody *else's!*"

He's got one foot in the grave and the other on a banana peel.

A real concern and worry of the farmer and the rancher is that if the country falls into a severe depression . . . how would they know?

"What became of the city feller you took on for your hired hand?"

"Well, before me he worked as a mechanic in town. So, when my mule balked, he climbed under it to see what was wrong!"

That feller couldn't find his rear end if it was on fire.

"My son took a job working on a farm in Costa Rica."

"Does he like it?"

"Not much. Kind of dangerous. He says he has to climb a ladder to milk the coconuts."

When they passed out brains, that fellow thought they said trains and got out of the way.

A city girl asked a farmer which term is correct, that a hen is "sitting" or "setting."

"It don't make me no difference," replied the farmer. "All that I want to know is whether she is 'laying' or 'lying'."

"It sure is a funny thing about chickens."

"Why's that?"

"Well, when you think about it, a chicken is the only critter you can eat before it's born."

A whistlin' gal and a crowin' hen are apt to come to no good end.

A farmer went to town to get medicines for his cow and for his wife. At the druggist's he told the attendant, "Be derned careful how you label them bottles. Write real plain which is fer the cow and which fer the wife. I sure don't want nothin' to happen to that cow."

A woman's love is like the morning dew. It is as likely to fall on a horse turd as upon a lily.

Farmer Jone's dairy barn had just burned down and the insurance agent was trying to explain that the policy allowed only rebuilding—just like the one destroyed—but that there could not be a cash settlement as Jones had requested.

And Jones was furious! "OK!" he bellowed, "if that's the kinda people you are, you can cancel the policy on my wife before it's too late!"

So I said to him, "Let's play horse. I'll play the head and you just be yourself!"

When George Lucas, the famous auctioneer, died impoverished, his obituary notice mentioned his great success
at selling farms and livestock. Then it soared into grandiose
language. "The dearly beloved George Lucas plunged into
the unfathomable, soared into the infinite, commenced with
the inscrutable, sang with heavenly songsters—but he never
paid cash."

He's so tight he can sit on a quarter and you can read
"E PLURIBUS UNUM" on his bottom.

Several Senators in the United States Senate were touting
the superiority of their states' products. Each state was the
acme of productivity—to hear them boast. And then the Senator of Missouri stood and addressed his colleagues as follows:
"If all our Missouri mules were made into one, he could rub
his ears against the North Pole, with his forefeet on the Aleu-
tians and Iceland, one hind foot on Havana and the other on
Panama; and, if he got riled, he could kick South American 73
miles beyond the South Pole; his hee-haw would make a
California earthquake sound like the rumble of one of Henry
Ford's old puddle-jumpers! and, if he was properly hitched, he
could pull Texas into the Republican Party."

He's so skinny he has to wear skis in the shower to keep
from goin' down the drain.

Things I'd Like to Know

Whether the ice plant grafted on a milk weed would make
ice-cream.
How the farmers keep the dust out of the potatoes' eyes.
Whether a detective could solve a garden plot.
Why the farmer allows the lambs to gambol on the green.
If it is dangerous to pass the buck on the farm.
Where the people hide when the bulrush's out.

If a mortgage is not a poor covering for a farm.
If it's dangerous to be out when the corn is shooting.
Whether an ill wind can cure hay.
Whether a farmer would be wise to sow wild oats.
What kind of straw a farmer uses for strawberries.
Whether a man roofing his barn is laying up something for a rainy day.
If a man always reaps what he sows.
If a chicken house and an egg-plant are the same.

Blaine C. Bigler

———————————

The mildest winter he ever spent was a summer in Minnesota.

———————————

"Ever hear tell of Nahum Welchcorn?" asked Milt Slemmons, tearing a splinter off the broom and cleaning out his pipestem.

"Well, sir, Nahum Welchcorn was the proud possessor of Slippery Caroline, the cussedest snake that ever lived.

"Nahum was an odd duffer. Very odd. He had queer ideas. It was queer that he should have ideas in the first place. When he had queer ones, that made it queerer yet. His queerest ideas was about snakes.

" 'Snakes,' he said, 'is harmless critters livin' in holes. Treat a snake right, and he'll do the right thing by you. Kick him in the shins, and he'll kick you back. Show him kindness and it'll bust your heart to see how pathetic he acts.'

"Snakes was his hobby. That ain't so dang strange to genealogists like me, because I remember that Nahum's father used to see snakes so often that he began to wish for 'em.

"It was hereditary with Nahum.

"Slippery Caroline was a bullsnake of the female denomination. It don't sound right, but that's the way with snakes. I don't like the dang things. Well, sir, that Caroline snake just slept and lived with Nahum, and she was no end to help around the place.

"She'd slip down a drain pipe and pull out the wad of hair that the hired girl dropped in. She'd crawl down under the sidewalk and bring up the dimes and quarters dropped through the cracks. She hunted the eggs, watched the cows and kept the rats out of the corncrib. She lived on scraps off the table.

"One time Nahum started out for a Sunday afternoon walk and fell through the ice in Pigeon Creek. Did he drown? Well, it looked like he would till Caroline got her massive brain a-working. She wrapped herself around a hickory stump and threw out her tail for a life-line and pulled Nahum ashore.

"Nahum hadn't any finer feelings and he never even got a cold out of it. But Caroline had a delicate constitution and she caught a cold in her throat. She died from that cold in her throat because they couldn't decide which part was her throat and didn't know where to put the mustard plaster.

Milt Clemmons, 1922

She's known as "Radio Station." Why? 'Cause anybody can pick her up.

Old Hen—"Let me give you a piece of good advice."
Young Hen—"What is it?"
Old Hen—"An egg a day keeps the ax away."

Statistics

Are you as deeply impressed as you once were with the barrels and firkins and kegs and kits and troughs and vats and bins and tubs of statistics some people are always ready to pull on you?

Did you ever halt one of those people afflicted with figuritis in the midst of one of his statistical hemorrhages and ask him how he knew it, and if he could prove it? And then, when he could prove it? And then, when he cited his authority, ask him if he knew where his authority got it?

Statistics are impressive largely in proportion as their sources are obscure and their falsity hard to establish.

There are some statistics that are true. Bound to be. Any

parboiled imbecile who wants to find our how many grains of wheat are in a pint and who wants to take a day off to count them, has that privilege. He can find out how many grains are in that pint, but he doesn't know how many grains, within a hundred or so, are in any other pint.

The average statistics are either rot, or run into such huge and un-understandable and un-graspable numbers that they practically are not numbers at all.

Any number over ten thousand or thereabouts might as well be squintillions so far as the capacity of the human mind incompassing the idea they represent goes.

The little facts that are in our hearts if we keep them clean and honest,—little facts that most of the big put-it-down-in-digits kind of facts are intended to counteract and disprove,— are as good as any.

Who cares for statistics when it comes to the really vital things?

The Bible says the hairs of our head are numbered, but it was kind enough not to tell us the number.

———————————

He's meaner than a two-stingered bumblebee crossed with a wasp.

———————————

"Is that a Texas milking machine?"

"Wul, we have driven 24 miles to the mail box to git a notice to drive 45 mile to town, to pay 3¢ postage due on a bill from the feed store!"

"Boy, I bet this ole country could shore look tough in a drought!"

Section 2

Abraham Lincoln's Farm Humor

No other human occupation opens so wide a field for profitable and agreeable combination of labor with cultivated thought as agriculture.

I feel like the girl who said, when she put on her stocking, "there's something in that worth looking into." (after going over plans for the Battleship Monitor.)

When asked how he liked being President, he said he felt like the man ridden out of town on a rail, tarred and feathered, who replied, "if it weren't for the honor of the thing I'd as soon walk."

I have come to the conclusion never again to think of marrying, and for this reason—I can never be satisfied with anyone who would be blockhead enough to have me. (In a letter dated 1838).

His description of a legal opponent: "He can compress the most words into the smallest idea of any man I ever met."

The President was harrassed by office-seekers. After he contracted Varioloid, a mild smallpox, he said; "Now I've got something to give everybody who comes for a job."

God must love the common people because he made so many of them.

Pres. Lincoln's description of a bothersome officeseeker: "That turkey-faced fellow! You would think he didn't know as much as a last year's bird's nest."

Advice to General Halleck: "Look out when you cross the river that you don't hang yourself in the middle like a steer on a fence, neither able to hook with your horns nor kick with your hooves."

It is almost certain . . . that by deeper plowing, analysis of soils, experiments with manure and varieties of seeds, observance of seasons, and the like, that causes [of falling yields] would be found.

Photograph provided by the
Illinois State Historic Preservation Agency

Introduction

Many Americans are unaware of the farm background of Abraham Lincoln that was the source of much of his strength, personality, wisdom and knowledge (horse sense).

His father, Thomas Lincoln, was a farmer although he was something less than able. He dawdled a lot! In fact, his contemporary described him as "a piddler," a man always busy but at nothing important. But a farmer he was, all of his life.

When Thomas Lincoln got ready for a wife, he sought her in the neighborhood of Elizabethtown, KY. He looked for a wife (as most farmers then did) with a "talent of hand." As they said, "a gal who could toss a pancake off a skillet up through the top of a chimney and run outside and catch it coming down." He found her in Nancy Hanks, the beloved mother of Abraham Lincoln.

Born February 12, 1809, Mr. Lincoln lived—boy and man— as a frontier countryman until he was 22 years old. Hence, his character, disposition, outlook on life and, most particularly, his sense of humor, grew from those formative years spent on and around frontier farms.

The hard work, sparse schooling, limited social life, arguments, feuds and brutal fights—together with the moral code of the frontier—all contributed to Mr. Lincoln's character. And the stories he heard there, especially as a lawyer on the 8th Judicial Circuit of Illinois, gave him a repertoire of sayings and tales that have come down to us from friends that knew him well. He told these stories in court and at night during social evenings at the small town taverns (hotels), and at political gatherings. He was to be a storyteller all his life.

Mr. Lincoln told stories not only to make or clarify a point, or clinch an argument, but for the sheer fun of it. Conversation, with storytelling, was the form of amusement most enjoyed back then. And Mr. Lincoln loved to tell stories on the farm, in towns, on the Circuit, in court, at political rallies and in cabinet meetings in the White House. Storytelling was simply an integral part of his talk, his speech; as natural as a smile to him.

He did not invent many stories but, rather, adapted the tales he read or heard to his own needs. Thus he was, in his own words, "a retail dealer," not an inventor, of his stories.

And he told stories so masterfully that people flocked to hear him during those evenings after court on the Judicial Circuit. Thus, his art at telling stories made him many political friends that could be counted on to vote for him when needed. And they did!

He used his 6' 4" thin body, with its long arms and legs, together with an usually mobile face and the gestures of an accomplished actor, to enchant his audiences. He would string-out a story, starting and stopping, moving about and grimacing until it came time for the "snapper" that sent them into paroxysms of laughter.

And he had a keen ear for dialect, a vital part of any versatile storyteller. His mimicking of German, Irish and Black dialect was superb and he loved to tell dialect stories.

Thus, the combination of an apt, funny story told by a masterful teller of tales so enchanted his listeners that, years after his death, those listeners remembered and remarked of his talent at "yarning."

Dirty stories? Of course, Most men told them and most adored them. Sex was as natural to the frontier as hands, head and feet. It went "with the territory" and talk about sex was common as Indians, bears and panthers.

When William Herndon, Mr. Lincoln's talented law partner was writing his excellent biography of Abraham Lincoln, he was advised not to include mention of his "swearing" because people would not believe he told such stories or used that kind of language. The advice was that to include such material would hurt the sales of the book! Doubtless, this attitude is responsible for so few of his "dirty" stories surviving to come down to us today.

His talent with funny stories was as much a part of his life as his talent at serious speaking as, e.g., The Gettysburg Address or his Second Inaugeral speech. Humor made life bearable on the frontier and during the racking, intense years in the White House during our Civil War. He said, "I laugh that I may not cry. That's all. That's all."

The most telling story, in terms of understanding Mr. Lincoln's love of humor, occured when a Congressman James Ashley came to the White House to see President Lincoln and demanded a certain action on a matter of grave urgency (to him).

"You have come up to see me about McClellan?"

"Yes sir!"

"Well," said the President, "that reminds me of a story."

"Mr. President, I beg your pardon, but I didn't come this morning to hear a story!"

"Ashley, I have great confidence in you, and great respect for you, and I know how sincere you are. But if I didn't tell these stories, I would die. Now you sit down."

Humanitarian, lawyer, competent soldier, exemplary human being, President of the United States, Abraham Lincoln was, also, a top-notch raconteur—teller of tales. Here are a few of his farm-related stories.

Photograph from the Illinois State Historical Library, with the help of
Thomas Schwartz, Curator, Abraham Lincoln Collection.

Young Abe Lincoln took a sack of grain to a mill whose proprietor was known as the laziest soul in Illinois. After watching the miller at work for a while, Abe commented drily, "I can eat that grain as fast as you're grinding it." "Indeed," grunted the miller. "And how long do you think you can keep that up?" "Until I starve to death," said Lincoln.

At the Illinois State House in 1858, Abraham Lincoln was discussing recent politics as practiced in the U.S. Congress. He told this story.

"Two old farmers living in the vicinity of Bloomington, had, from time immemorial, been at loggerheads. They could never agree, except to disagree; wouldn't build division fences; and, in short, were everlastingly quarreling. One day, one of them got over to the land of the other; the parties met, and a regular pitched battle between them was the consequence. The one who came out second best sued the other for assault and battery, and I was sent for to come up and defend the suit.

"Among the witnesses for the plaintiff was a remarkably talkative old fellow, who was disposed to magnify the importance of the affair to my client's disadvantage. It came my turn to question him:

"Witness," said I, "you say you saw this fight."

"Yes, stranger; I reckon I did."

"Was it much of a fight?" said I.

"I'll be darned if it wasn't, stranger; a right smart fight."

"How much ground did the combatants cover?"

"About an acre, stranger,"

"About an acre," I repeated, musingly.

"Well, now, witness, just tell me, wasn't that just about the smallest crop of a fight off of an acre of ground that ever you heard of?"

"That's so, stranger; I'll be gol darned if it wasn't!"

"The jury," added [AL], giving his legs an additional twist, after the crowd had finished laughing at the application of the anecdote—"the jury fined my client just ten cents!"

All of Mr. Lincoln's cronies in Illinois knew of his early and impoverished boyhood on farms of Kentucky and Indiana. And so they understood the following story he told during the Lincoln-Douglas debates in 1848. Douglas had paid Mr. Lincoln a compliment and this was his response to the flattery.

"I was not very much accustomed to flattery, and it came the sweeter to me. I was rather like the Hoosier, with the gingerbread, when he said he reckoned he loved it better than any other man, and got less of it."

Americans today think of Abraham Lincoln as handsome. in his day he was not so considered. And the following story indicates that he himself did not consider himself handsome.

"A yarn is told of him that on one occasion he was splitting rails, with only shirt and breeches on collar open and in that plight was not very likely to look at a man happened to be passing with a gun, called to Lincoln to look up, which he did. The man raised his gun in a attitude to shoot. Says Lincoln: What do you mean? The man replied that he had promised to shoot the first man he meet who was uglier than himself. Lincoln asked to see the man's face and after taking a look remarked, If I am uglier than you, then blaze away, opening his shirt bosom."

In the 1860's, during Abraham Lincoln's days as President, Illinois was a new country. Its rich soil, the richest in the world, only just beginning to be recognized by the American people as just that. It was a mixture of superb prairie begging for the plow and swampy areas begging for tile drainage. Into this situation came an itinerant preacher who wanted to use the hall of the House of Illinois Representatives for a religious lecture. "And just what is the subject of your lecture?" asked the officer in charge of the Hall, Jesse Dubois, the State Auditor. "The Second Coming of Christ," said the preacher.

"The Second Coming!" roared Dubois. "Hell fire, preacher,

if Christ had been to Springfield once and got away, he'd be damned clear of coming again."

President Lincoln and a group of friends were discussing the Presidential aspirations of Salmon P. Chase, one of the Cabinet officers. President Lincoln compared the man's hopes to a horsefly on the neck of a plowhorse, more gadfly than a horsefly in that it kept him eagerly working. He told this story.

"My brother and I . . . were once ploughing corn on a Kentucky farm, I driving the horse, and he holding the plough. The horse was lazy; but on one occasion rushed across the field so that I, with my long legs, could scarcely keep pace with him. On reaching the end of the furrow, I found an enormous *chin fly* fastened upon him, and knocked him off. My brother asked me what I did that for. I told him I didn't want the old horse bitten in that way. 'Why,' said my brother, *'that's all that made him go!'* "Now," said Mr. Lincoln, "if Mr. [Chase] has a presidential *chin fly* biting him, I'm not going to knock him off, if it will only make his department [the Treasury] *go.*"

Mr. Lincoln was fond of telling this story about a good friend of his, a fellow lawyer on the Eighth Judicial Circuit of Illinois. The good friend, Usher F. Linder, had managed, after a long, hard trial, to get a client acquitted of a charge of stealing a hog. His advice to his client was to go get a drink. "But," said Usher, "my advice to you is to drink the water of Tennessee because water in Tennessee is safer for you."

Abraham Lincoln did not drink whiskey although most of the lawyers on the Circuit did drink it. One of the heavier drinkers was Leonard Swett, about whom this story is told.

"I attended court many years ago at Mt. Pulaski, the first county seat of Logan County, and there was the jolliest set of rollicking young Lawyers there that you ever saw together. There was Bill Ficklin, Bill Herndon, Leonard Swett and a lot more, and they mixed law and Latin, water and whiskey, with equal success. It so fell out that the whiskey seemed to be possessed of the very spirit of Jonah. At any rate, Swett went out to the hog-pen, and, leaning over, began to 'throw up Jonah.' The hogs evidently thought it feed time, for they rushed forward and began to squabble over the voided matter.

" 'Don't fight (hic),' said Swett; 'There's enough (hic) for all.' "

In 1863, President Lincoln was terribly burdened with office-seekers. His waiting room was full of men from all over the Union and each was certain that his efforts alone enabled the President to be elected. One day, Mr. Lincoln told the assembled hopefuls this story.

"Gentlemen, I must tell you a little story I read one day when I was minding a mudscow in one of the bayous near the Yazoo. A certain king had a minister upon whose judgment he always depended, just as I do upon my friend here," pointing to me, said Seward, blushing.

"Now it happened that one day the king took it into his head to go a hunting, and after summoning his nobles and making the necessary preparations, he summoned the minister and asked him if it would rain. The minister told him it would not, and he and his nobles departed.

"While journeying along they met a countryman on a jackass. He advised them to return. 'For,' said he, 'it will certainly rain.' They smiled contemptuously upon him and passed on. Before they had gone many miles, however, they had reason to regret not having taken the rustic's advice, as a heavy shower coming up, they were drenched to the skin.

"When they had returned to the palace the king reprimanded the minister severely.

" 'I met a countryman,' said he, 'and he knows a great deal more than you, for he told me it would rain, whereas you told me it would not.'

"The king gave him his walking papers, and sent for the countryman, who made his appearance.

" 'Tell me,' said the king, 'how you knew it would rain?'

" 'I didn't know,' said the rustic, 'my jackass told me.'

" 'And how, pray, did he tell you?' asked the king.

" 'By pricking up his ears, your majesty,' returned the rustic.

"The king sent the countryman away, and procuring the jackass of him, put him (the jackass) in the place the minister had filled.

"And here," observed Mr. Lincoln, looking very wise, "is where the king made a great mistake."

"How so?" inquired his auditors eagerly.

"Why, ever since that time," said Mr. Lincoln, with a grin, "every jackass wants an office!"

President Lincoln told the story of an acquaintance who got elected to the legislature, and was almost too proud of his feat. He became somewhat pompous and began to use big words.

On the farm of this fellow there was a large and dangerous bull called Big Brindle and this bull frequently broke down fences and generally made a pest of itself.

One day the legislator called his hired man, the supervisor of the farm and told him to "impound Big Brindle in order that I may hear no animadversions on his eternal depredations."

The hired man did as he was told. But he wanted to respond to the inevitable query as to what he had done about Big Brindle, in the same high fallutin' way as the boss had addressed him.

So one evening, in the presence of a large number of quests, the boss asked the hired man if he had "impounded Big Brindle."

The man replied as follows: "Yes, I did, sir, but old Brindle transcended the impannel of the impound and scatterlophisticated all over the equanimity of the forest."

"What do you mean by that, sir!" roared the boss.

"Why, I mean, Sir, that old Brindle, being prognosticated with an idea of the cholera, ripped and teared, snorted and pawed, jumped the fence, tuck to the woods and would not be impounded nohow."

The boss, guests and all burst into laughter and the hired man went off, thinking to himself: "I reckon the boss won't ask me to impound any more cattle."

In the White House was a visitor who congratulated Mr. Lincoln on the prospects of his re-election. He was answered by that indefatigable storyteller with an anecdote of an Illinois farmer, who undertook to blast his own rocks. His first effort at producing an explosion proved a failure. He explained the cause by exclaiming, "Pshaw, this powder has been shot before."

In answer to a curiosity seeker who desired a permit to pass the lines to visit the field of Bull-Run after the first battle in July, 1861, Mr. Lincoln told this story:

A man in Cortlandt country raised a porker of such unusual size that strangers went out of their way to see it. One of them the other day met the old gentleman and inquired about the animal. 'Wall, yes,' the old fellow said; 'he'd got such a critter, mighty big un; but he guessed he would have to charge him about a shillin' for lookin' at him.' The stranger looked at the old man for a minute or so; pulled out the desired coin, handed it to him and started to go off. 'Hold on,' said the other, 'don't you want to see the hog?' 'No,' said the stranger, 'I have seen as big a hog as I want to see!'

And you will find that fact the case yourself, if you should happen to see a few *live* rebels there as well as dead ones.

A crony of Mr. Lincoln's, a man named Payne, was appointed a general at Illinois; in reference to his election the following is recorded, which the president tells with great *gusto*: One day a wealthy old lady, whose plantation was in the vicinity of the camp, came in and inquired for General Payne. When the commander made his appearance, the old lady in warm language told him that his men had stolen her last coop of chickens, and demanded its restoration or its value in money. "I am sorry for you, madam," replied the general, "but I can't help it. The fact is, madam, we are determined to squelch out the rebellion, if it cost every d——d chicken in Tennessee."

Abraham Lincoln told the following story in reference to some opposing candidates who had claimed to be exceptional fellows. This story is how he handled such conceit.

"There was an old Baptist Preacher,—the meeting house was way off in the woods from any other house, and was only used once a month; this preacher was dressed in coarse linen pants, and shirt of the same material; the pants were made after the old fashion, with big bag legs and but one button to the waistbands, and two flap buttons, no suspenders; and the shirt had crimp sleeves and one button on the collar. He raised up in the Pulpit and took his Text, thus: I am the Christ whom I shall represent to-day; about this time one of these blue Lizards or scorpions ran up his legs; the old man began to slap away on his legs, but missed the Lizard, and kept getting higher up, he unbuttoned his pants at one snatch, and kicked off his pants, but the thing kept on up his back; the next motion was for the collar button of his shirt, and off it went. In the house was an old Lady, who took a good look at him, and said, 'well, if you represent Christ, I am done believing in the Bible.'" This anecdote he told somewhere in his speech, in reply to some of the opposite candidates, who had represented themselves something extra.

A Charles F. Hart visited Mr. Lincoln in 1863 and, among other subjects discussed was the one about officers in the army. Mr. Hart remarked that too many men wanted to be officers who were unfit to serve. Then President Lincoln told this story.

"Yes, it is so. That reminds me of a story I heard in a small town in Illinois where I once lived. Every man in town owned a fast horse, each one considering his own the fastest, so to decide the matter there was to be a trial of all the horses to take place at the same time. One old man living in the town known as "Uncle" was selected as umpire; when it was over and each one anxious for his decision, the old man putting his hands behind his back said "I have come to one conclusion, that where there are so many fast horses in our little town, none of them are any great shakes."

A Western farmer sought the President day after day until he procured the much desired audience. He had a plan for the successful prosecution of the war, to which Mr. Lincoln listened as patiently as he could. When he was through, he asked the opinion of the President upon his plan. "Well," said Mr. Lincoln, "I'll answer by telling you a story. You have heard of Mr. Blank, of Chicago? He was an immense loafer in his way—in fact, never did anything in his life. One day he got crazy over a great rise in the price of wheat, upon which many wheat speculators gained large fortunes. Blank started off one morning to one of the most successful of the wheat speculators, and with much enthusiasm laid before him a plan by which he (the said Blank) was certain of becoming independently rich. When he had finished, he asked the opinion of his hearer upon his plan of operations. The reply came as follows: 'My advice is that you stick to your business.' 'But,' asked Blank, 'What is my business?' 'I don't know, I am sure, what it is,' says the merchant; 'but whatever it is, I advise you to stick to it.' "

It was, perhaps, in connection with the newspaper attacks, that he told, during the sitting [2 March 1865], this story.—"A traveller on the frontier found himself out of his reckoning one night in a most inhospitable region. A terrific thunder-storm came up, to add to his trouble. He floundered along until his horse at length gave out. The lightning afforded him the only clew of his way, but the peals of thunder were frightful. One bolt, which seemed to crash the earth beneath him, brought him to his knees. By no means a praying man, his petition was short and to the point,— "O Lord, if it is all the same to you, give us a little more light and a little less noise."

There is an anecdote about how Lincoln as a young surveyor, stayed overnight at the farm of a transplanted Pennsylvanian and told stories around the fireplace.

"When I was a little boy, I lived in the State of Kentucky where drunkenness was very common on election days; at an election in a village near where I lived, on a day when the weather was inclement and the roads exceedingly muddy, a toper named Bill got brutally drunk and staggered down a narrow alley where he layed himself down in the mud, and remained there until the dusk of the evening, at which time he recovered from his stupor; finding himself very muddy—immediately started for the town pump to wash himself.

On his way to the pump another drunken man was leaning over a fence post. Bill mistook him for the pump and at once took hold of the arm mistaking it for the handle, the use of which set the other drunk to throwing up; Bill, believing all was right, put both hands under the cascading vomit and gave himself a thorough washing. He then made his way to the grocery for something to drink. On entering the door one of his comrades exclaimed in a tone of surprise, "Why, Bill, what in the world is the matter?" Bill said in reply, "By God, you ought to have seen me before I was washed."

I feel, said Lincoln—jokingly—like a little neighbor boy of mine in Indiana—his father was a hunter—he was tender and chicken hearted; his father one night caught an old coon and her young—killed the old one and all the young except one—tied a little rope around the neck of it, and told the boy to watch it while he, the father, went and got a chain—and the boy was afraid his father would treat it cruelly—Lincoln went over to see the boy—the boy was apparently crying—was tender—never would throw at a bird—said to Abe—"I wish this Coon would get away—, but if I let him go, dad will whip me—, I do wish it would run off—." So I feel by these leading rebels—Davis,

Lee &c. I wish they could get away—yet if I let 'em loose—dad—the People would whip me—and yet I do wish they would run away out of the land."

The Union was fearful of foreign intervention, especially Great Britain. President Lincoln told this story, probably to illustrate past British attitudes!

"It appears that shortly after we had peace with England Mr. (Ethan) Allen had occasion to visit England, and while their the English took Great pleasure in teasing him, and trying to make fun of the Americans and General Washington in particular And one day they got a picture of General Washington, and hung it up the Back House where Mr. Allen could see it.

"And they finally asked Mr. A. if he saw that picture of his friend in the Back House.

"Mr. Allen said No, but said he thought that it was very appropriate for an Englishman to keep it. Why they asked, for said Mr. Allen, there is Nothing that will make an Englishman SHIT so quick as the Sight of Genl Washington And after that they let Mr. Allen [and] Washington alone."

Mr. Lincoln was appointed by the District Court to defend a man involved in what seemed to be a hopeless case. And throughout the trial, the hopelessness of his cause seemed to be more and more confirmed. Then Lincoln made his concluding appeal to the jury with these words: "My worthy friend, the prosecuting attorney, has made a good try. But let me tell you this . . . he's got his facts right but his conclusions are wrong."

When the jury heard this, they burst out laughing, they retired to consider judgment. They returned to court with the finding that the defendant was NOT GUILTY!

Everyone in the courtroom was astonished. But the most puzzled by the verdict was the prosecuting attorney who took Mr. Lincoln aside and demanded to know what had happened. "I had this case won hands down," the Prosecuting Attorney said. "Everybody knew it. Then you come along with some foolish words like, 'He's got his facts right but his conclusions are wrong', and the jury busts a gut laughing and says: 'not guilty'. Now, how come, Lincoln! What does it all mean?"

"You should have been at the tavern last night," Mr. Lincoln told him. "Then you'd understand."

"I've got relatives here," the prosecuting attorney said. "We had dinner together and then retired."

"Just so," nodded Mr. Lincoln. "But almost the whole town was there, including the folks on the jury. Well, we were all telling stories, having a good time, and I told them the story of the little farm kid, Johnny, who came running into the house to tell his daddy: "Papa! Papa! Come quick! Sister Mary is up in the hay loft with the hired man and she's got her skirts up and he's got his pants down and they're fixin' to pee all over our new hay."

"Well," continued Lincoln, "the old farmer stroked his beard and looked at his son and then said: "Sonny, you got your facts right but your conclusions wrong!""

"And that," said Mr. Lincoln, "is what I told the jury and with that I won the case!"

"Mr. President," said a friend to him, "there isn't much left of [Confederate General J.B.] Hood's army [defeated December 1864], is there?"

"Well, no, Medill, I think Hood's army is about in the fix of Bill Sykes's dog, down in Sangamon county. Did you ever hear it?"

Of course, the answer was, "Never."

"Well, Bill Sykes had a long, *yaller* dog, that was forever getting into the neighbors' meat-houses and chicken-coops. They had tried to kill it a hundred times, but the dog was always too smart for them. Finally, one of them got a bladder of a coon, and filled it up with powder, tying the neck around a piece of punk. When he saw the dog coming he fired the punk, split open a hot biscuit and put the bladder in, then buttered all nicely and threw it out. The dog swallored it at a gulp.

Pretty soon there was an explosion. The head of the dog lit on the porch, the fore-legs caught astraddle the fence, the hind-legs fell in the ditch, and the rest of the dog lay around loose. Pretty soon Bill Sykes came along, and the neighbor said: 'Bill, I guess there ain't much of that dog of your'n left.' 'Well, no,' said Bill; 'I see plenty of pieces, but I guess that dog, *as a dog*, ain't of much more account.' Just so, Medill, there may be fragments of Hood's army around, but I guess that dog, *as a dog*, ain't of much more account."

General R. C. Schenks discovered that, in his efforts to recruit blacks for his army, he could not tell the free blacks from those who had run away from their masters. He asked Mr. Lincoln for instructions on what he should do. The President's response was as follows:

"You see, Schenck," said Mr. Lincoln, "we are like an old acquaintance of mine who settled on a piece of *'galled'* prairie. It was a terrible rough place to clear up; but after a while he got a few things growing—here and there a patch of corn, a few hills of beans, and so on. One day a stranger stopped to look at his place, and wanted to know how he managed to cultivate so rough a spot. 'Well,' was the reply, 'some of it is pretty rough. The smaller stumps I can generally root out or burn out; but now and then there is an old settler that bothers me, and there is no other way but to plough around it.' "Now, Schenck," Mr. Lincoln concluded, "at such a time as this, troublesome cases are constantly coming up, and the only way to get along at all is to plough around them."

During the Civil War there was considerable concern that we might work ourselves into a war on two fronts, with the South and with Great Britain. When asked what he thought of the dangerous possibilities of the situation, Pres. Lincoln replied as follows:

"My father," he said, "had a neighbor from whom he was only separated by a fence. On each side of that fence there were two savage dogs, who kept running backward and forward along the barrier all day, barking and snapping at each other. One day they came to a large opening recently made in the fence. Perhaps you think they took advantage of this to devour each other? Not at all; scarcely had they seen the gap, when they both ran back, each on his own side, with their tails between their legs. These two dogs are fair representatives of America and England."

In the summer of 1862, a delegation complained about the conduct of the war in the West. Pres. Lincoln rose from his chair and said, Judge List, this reminds me of an anedcote which I heard a son of yours tell in Burlington in Iowa. He was trying to enforce upon his hearers the truth of the old adage that three moves is worse than a fire. As an illustration he gave an account of a family who started from Western Pennsylvania, pretty well off in this world's goods when they started. But they moved and moved, having less and less every time they moved, till after a while they could carry every thing in one wagon. He said that the chickens of the family got so used to being moved, that whenever they saw the wagon sheets brought out they laid themselves on their backs and crossed their legs, ready to be tied. Now, gentlemen, if I were to listen to every committee that comes in at that door, I had just as well cross my hands and let you tie me."

Mr. Lincoln illustrated his concern over a proposed tariff by telling this story:

"A revenue we must have. In order to keep house, we must have breakfast, dinner and supper; and this tariff business seems to be necessary to bring them. But yet, there is something obscure about it. It reminds me of the fellow that came into a grocery down here in Menard County, at Salem, where I once lived, and called for a picayune's worth of crackers; so the clerk laid them out on the counter. After sitting awhile, he said to the clerk, 'I don't want these crackers, take them, and give me a glass of cider.' So the clerk put the crackers back into the box, and handed the fellow the cider. After drinking, he started for the door. 'Here, Bill,' called out the clerk, 'pay me for your cider.' 'Why,' said Bill, 'I gave you the crackers for it.' 'Well, then, pay me for the crackers.' 'But I hain't had any;' responded Bill. 'That's so,' said the clerk. "Well, clear out! It seems to me that I've lost a picayune somehow, but I can't make it out exactly.' " So," said Lincoln, after the laugh had subsided, "it is with the tariff; somebody gets the picayune, but I don't exactly understand how."

The politician, Weed, once joked that his appetite for sausage depended on whether pork was cheaper than dogs. "That," said Mr. Lincoln, "reminds me of what occurred down at Joliet, where a popular grocer supplied all the villages with sausages. One Saturday evening, when his grocery was filled with customers, for whom he and his boys were busily engaged in weighing sausages, a neighbor, with whom he had had a violent quarrel that day, came into the grocery, made his way up to the counter, holding two enormous dead cats by the tail, which he deliberately threw on the counter, saying, "This makes seven to-day. I'll call around on Monday and get my money for them."

[Titian J. Coffey, assistant attorney general in 1863, recalled this story, when he told the President that U.S. marshals preferred to tap a legal defense fund rather than seek aid from district attorneys:] "Yes," said he, "they will now all be after the money and be content with nothing else. They are like the man in Illinois, whose cabin was burned down, and according to the kindly custom of early days in the West, his neighbors all contributed something to start him again. In his case they had been so liberal that he soon found himself better off than before the fire, and he got proud. One day, a neighbor brought him a bag of oats, but the fellow refused it with scorn. 'No,' said he, 'I'm not taking oats now, I take nothing but money.' "

He and a certain Judge once got to bantering one another about trading horses; and it was agreed that the next morning at nine o'clock they should make a trade, the horse to be unseen up to that hour,—and no backing out, under a forfeit of twenty-five dollars. At the hour appointed, the Judge came up, leading the sorriest looking specimen of a nag ever seen in those parts. In a few minutes Mr. Lincoln was seen approaching with a *wooden sawhorse* upon his shoulders. Great were the shouts and the laughter of the crowd; and these increased, when Mr. Lincoln, surveying the Judge's animal, set down his sawhorse, and exclaimed: "Well, Judge, this is the first time I ever *got the worst of it* in a horse-trade!"

———————

William Herndon, Lincoln's law partner and biographer, told this story about a group of Democrats, called Locofocos, who claimed to be the true descendants of the Founding Fathers but who, said Mr. Lincoln, were frauds as in this story:

Once an old farmer in the Country heard a devil of a racket in his hen house—heard it often before, so he thought to get up and see what was the matter and kill this thing, if it was some wild animal. He got up—lit his candle and went gun in hand—to see and fight it out. On going into the hen house he looked around on the floor & in the roosts and at last found his enemy, a pole cat crouched in the corner with two or three dead chickens. The farmer seized the pole cat and dragged him out and all who know the nature of such a cat know what followed—a devil of a stink. The pole cat demurred as well as he could on his own language saying that he was no such brute as charged, but an innocent animal and a friend of the farmer just come to take care of his chickens. The farmer to this replied—"You look like a pole cat—just the size of a pole cat—act like one," snuffing up his nose "and smell like one and you are one by God, and I'll kill you, innocent & as friendly to me as you say you are." "These locofocos," said Lincoln "claim to be true democrats, but they are only locofocos—they look like locofocos—just the size of locofocos—act like locofocos—and" turning up his nose and backing away a little on the Stand as if the smell was about to smother him "are locofocos by God."

In Coles County, Illinois, in 1850, Abraham Lincoln was assigned, by the court, to defend a man accused of stealing hogs. The man showed superb confidence in being acquitted and Mr. Lincoln did, in fact, win the case. Curious as to how the man could be so certain of winning the case, Mr. Lincoln took him aside and asked for an explanation. The man obliged him and explained as follows:

"Well, Lincoln, my good fellow, I'll tell you. I did steal the hogs and more of 'em than I was indicted for—many more and sold 'em to my neighbors, the jury: They knew that if I was convicted that they would have to pay for the hogs that I sold 'em, as they belonged to Mr. —— and Mr. —— and the jury knew it from the evidence. Now, Lincoln, do you see where the joke comes in? I knew that I would be cleared—didn't I tell you so." Lincoln was astonished at the fellow & his story: he used to tell the story on circuit with great gusto and to the delight of his brother attys of the bar.

Pres. Lincoln was discussing with Ordance Officers, a new gun powder then in preparation for use in 15 inch cannon.

"Well, it's rather larger than the powder we used to buy in my shooting days. It reminds me of what occurred once in a country meeting-house in Sangamon County. You see, there were very few newspapers then, and the country storekeepers had to resort to some other means of advertising their wares. If, for instance, the preacher happened to be late in coming to a prayer-meeting of an evening, the shopkeepers would often put in the time while the people were waiting by notifying them of any new arrival of an attractive line of goods. One evening a man rose up and said 'Bretheren, let me take occasion to say, while we're a-waitin', that I have jest received a new inv'ice of sportin' powder. The grains are so small you kin sca'cely see 'em with the naked eye, and polished up so fine you kin stand up and comb yer ha'r in front of one o' them grains jest like it was a lookin' glass. Hope you'll come down to my store at the cross-roads and examine that powder for yourselves.' When he had got about this far a rival powder-merchant in the meeting, who had been boiling over with indignation at the amount of advertising the opposition powder was getting, jumped up and cried out: 'Brethren, I hope you'll not believe a single word Brother Jones has been sayin' about that powder. I've been down thar and seen it for myself, and I pledge you my word that the grains is bigger than the lumps in a coal-pile; and any one of you, brethren, ef you was in your future state, could put a bar'l o' that powder on your shoulder and march squar' through the sulphurious flames surroundin' you without the least danger of an explosion.' "

Judge H. W. Beckwith, in his "Personal Recollections of Lincoln," offers an example of Lincoln's ability to "condense the law and the facts of an issue in a story":

"A man, by vile words, first provoked and then made a bodily attack upon another. The latter, in defending himself, gave the other much the worst of the encounter. The agressor, to get even, had the one who thrashed him tried in our Circuit Court on a charge of an assault and battery. Mr. Lincoln defended, and told the jury that his client was in the fix of a man who, in going along the highway with a pitchfork on his shoulder, was attacked by a fierce dog that ran out at him from a farmer's dooryard. In parrying off the brute with the fork, its prongs stuck into the brute and killed him.

" 'What made you kill my dog?' said the farmer.

" 'What made him try to bite me?'

" 'But why did you not go at him with the other end of the pitchfork?'

" 'Why did he not come after me with his other end?' "

Pres. Lincoln was discussing the extravagant brags of some of the Union officers:

"These fellows remind me of the fellow who owned a dog

which, so he said, just hungered and thirsted to combat and eat up wolves. It was a difficult matter, so the owner declared, to keep that dog from devoting the entire twenty-four hours of each day to the destruction of his enemies. He just 'hankered' to get at them.

"One day a party of this dog-owner's friends thought to have some sport. These friends heartily disliked wolves, and were anxious to see the dog eat up a few thousand. So they organized a hunting party and invited the dog-owner and the dog to go with them. They desired to be personally present when the wolf-killing was in progress.

"It was noticed that the dog-owner was not over-enthusiastic in the matter; he pleaded a 'business engagement,' but as he was the most notorious and torpid of the town loafers, and wouldn't have recognized a 'business engagement' had he met it face to face, his excuse was treated with contempt. Therefore he had to go.

"The dog, however, was glad enough to go, and so the party started out. Wolves were in plenty, and soon a pack was discovered, but when the 'wolfhound' saw the ferocious animals he lost heart, and, putting his tail between his legs, endeavored to slink away. At last—after many trials—he was enticed into the small growth of underbrush where the wolves had secreted themselves, and yelps of terror betrayed the fact that the battle was on.

"Away flew the wolves, the dog among them, the hunting party following on horseback. The wolves seemed frightened, and the dog was restored to public favor. It really looked as if he had the savage creatures on the run, as he was fighting heroically when last sighted.

"Wolves and dog soon disappeared, and it was not until the party arrived at a distant farmhouse that news of the combatants was gleaned.

" 'Have you seen anything of a wolf-dog and a pack of wolves around here?' was the question anxiously put to the male occupant of the house, who stood idly leaning upon the gate.

" 'Yep,' was the short answer.

" 'How were they going?'

" 'Purty fast,'

" 'What was their position when you saw them?'

" 'Well,' replied the farmer, in a most exasperatingly deliberate way. 'The dog was a leetle bit ahead.' "

"That reminds me of a fellow out in Illinois, who has better luck in getting prairie chickens than any one in the neighborhood. He had a rusty old gun no other man dared to handle; he never seemed to exert himself, being listless and indifferent went out after game, but he always brought home all the chickens he could carry, while some of the others, with their finely trained dogs and latest improved fowling-pieces, came home alone.

" 'How is it, Jake?' inquired one sportsman, who, although a good shot, and knew something about hunting, was often unfortunate, 'that you never come home without a lot of birds?'

"Jake grinned, half-closed his eyes, and replied: 'Oh, I don't know that there's anything queer about it. I jes' go ahead an' git' em.'

" 'Yes, I know you do; but how do you do it?'

" 'You'll tell.'

" 'Honest, Jake, I won't say a word. Hope to drop dead this minute.'

" 'Never say nothing, if I tell you?'

" 'Cross my heart three times.'

"This reassured Jake, who put his mouth close to the ear of his eager questioner, and said, in a whisper: 'All you got to do is jes' to hide in a fence corner an' make a noise like a turnip. That'll bring the chickens every time.'"

During one of his visits to Chicago he was the guest of a friend whose residence was in the fashionable part of the city. It was in the summer of 1858 and about the time of the campaign with Douglas. He was sitting with his host and family on the front veranda facing a small park one evening when he noticed among the children a little fellow who was fat and exceptionally short of stature. "That boy," he observed roguishly, "reminds me of a man named Moore in Springfield, who suffered the loss of both feet in a railroad accident and whose legs are now so short that when he walks in the snow the seat of his trousers wipes up his footprints."

One day in the summer of 1857 Abraham Lincoln was sitting in his office when he was visited by one of his neighbors, an excellent farmer, but one inclined to increase the size of his crops even after harvesting. He had given on this particular morning a skillfully padded account of the hay he had put in. "I've been cutting hay, too," remarked Mr. Lincoln. "Why, Abe, are you farming?" "Yes." "What you raise?" "Just hay." "Good crop this year?" "Excellent." "How many tons?" "Well, I don't know just how many tons, Simpson, but my men stacked all they could outdoors and then stored the rest in the barn."

Mr. Lincoln enjoyed the description of how this Congressman led the race from Bull's Run, and laughed at it heartily. "I never knew but one fellow who could run like that," he said, "and he was a young man out in Illinois. He had been sparking a girl, much against the wishes of her father. In fact, the old man took such a dislike to him that he threatened to shoot him if he ever caught him around his premises again.

"One evening the young man learned that the girl's father had gone to the city, and he ventured out to the house. He was sitting in the parlor, with his arm around Betsy's waist, when he suddenly spied the old man coming around the corner of the house with a shotgun. Leaping through a window into the garden, he started down a path at the top of his speed. He was a long-legged fellow, and could run like greased lightning. Just then a jack-rabbit jumped up in the path in front of him. In about two leaps he overtook the rabbit. Giving it a kick that sent it high in the air, he exclaimed: 'Git out of the road, gosh dern you, and let somebody run that knows how.' "

There was a Methodist minister in a farm area of Kansas, living on a small salary, who was greatly troubled to get his quarterly installment. He at last told the non-paying trustees, farmers all, that he must have his money, as he was suffering for the necessities of life.

"Money!" replied the trustees, "you preach for money? We thought you preached for the good of souls!"

"Souls!" responded the reverend, "I can't eat souls; and if I could it would take a thousand such as yours to make a meal!"

The President was plagued with demands that General U.S. Grant be sacked, fired, removed. He responded to the demands with this story:

"Out in my State of Illinois there was a man nominated for sheriff of the county. He was a good man for the office, brave, determined and honest, but not much of an orator. In fact, he couldn't talk at all; he couldn't make a speech to save his life.

"His friends knew he was a man who would preserve the peace of the country and perform the duties devolving upon him all right, but the people of the county didn't know it. They wanted him to come out boldly on the platform at political meetings and state his convictions and principles; they had been used to speeches from candidates, and were somewhat suspicious of a man who was afraid to open his mouth.

"At last the candidate consented to make a speech, and his friends were delighted. The candidate was on hand, and, when he was called upon, advanced to the front and faced the crowd. There was a glitter in his eye that wasn't pleasing, and the way he walked out to the front of the stand showed that he knew just what he wanted to say.

" 'Feller Citizens,' was his beginning, the words spoken quietly, 'I'm not a speakin' man; I ain't no orator, an' I never stood up before a lot of people in my life before; I'm not goin' to make no speech, 'xcept to say that I can lick any man in the crowd!' "

———————————

He related the following story to illustrate that he perfectly well knew what was at stake. He saw that while Douglas, a "trimmer," might win the lesser office, U.S. Senator, he would damn himself for the prospect of being the next President. It so fell out.

"There was an old farmer out our way, who had a fair daughter and a fine apple tree, each of which he prized as 'the apple of his eye.'

"One of the courters 'sparking' up for her hand was a dashing young fellow, while his rival next in consequence was but a plain person in face and speech, whom, however, the farmer favored, no doubt from 'Like liking Like.' (The dashing young chap was afterwards hanged, by the way.) One day, the two happened to meet at the farmer's fence. It enclosed this orchard where the famous Baldwin flourished. That year was the off-year, but, as somewhiles occurs, the yield, though sparse, comprised some rare beauties. There was one, a 'whopper,' on which the farmer had centered his care as if for a human pet. He looked after it well, and saw it heave up into plumpness with joy. When Dashing Jack came up, he saw his fellow-beau just hefting a stone.

" 'What are you going to do with that rock?' asked he, careless-like, though somehow or other interested, too, as we are in anything a rival does in the neighborhood of our sweetheart.

" 'Why, I was just a-going to see if I could knock off that big red apple, that is all.'

" 'You can't do it in the first try?' taunted the dasher.

" 'Neither can you. Bet!'

"Jack would not make any bet with plain John, but he took up a pebble and, contemputuously whistling through his fine regular teeth, shied, and, sure as fate! knocked the big Baldwin in the girth and sent it hopping off the limb. Then, as the victors are entitled to the spoil, he went in, picked up the fruit, and was walking up to the house when whom should he run up against but the old man! Now, to see that apple off, and to see any man munching it like a crab, was too much for his nerves. He did not stop to say 'Meal or Flour?' but, wearing these here copper-toed boots such as were a novelty in that section 'bout then, he raised the young man so that he and the apple, to which he clung, landed this side of the fence together, in two-two's.

"Then? Well! then, the plain John swallowed a snicker or two, and went right in, condoled with the old fellow on his loss of the pet Baldy, and asked for the girl right slick.

"Dashing Jack got the apple, but it was t'other *who got the gal.*"

A balloon ascension occurred in New Orleans "befo' de wa'," and after sailing in the air several hours, the aeronaut, who was arrayed in silks and spangles like a circus performer, descended in a cotton field, where a gang of slaves were at work. The frightened negroes took to the woods—all but one venerable darkey, who was rheumatic and could not run, and who, as the resplendent aeronaut approached, having apparently just dropped from heaven, said: "Good mawning, Massa Jesus; how's your Pa?"

France had called for an international conference of Great Britain, Russia and France to mediate America's Civil War. To illustrate American attitude toward this meddlesome venture, President Lincoln told this story:

"Just before we left Indiana and crossed into Illinois," Mr. Lincoln said solemnly, speaking in a grave tone of voice, "we came across a small farm-house full of nothing but children. These ranged in years from seventeen years to seventeen months, and all were in tears. The mother of the family was red-headed and red-faced, and the whip she held in her right hand led to the inference that she had been chastising her brood. The father of the family, a meek-looking, mild mannered, tow-headed chap, was standing in the front door-way, awaiting—to all appearances—his turn to feel the thong.

"I thought there wasn't much use in asking the head of that house if she wantd any 'notions.' She was too busy. It was evident an insurrection had been in progress, but it was pretty well quelled when I got there. The mother had about suppressed it with an iron hand, but she was not running any risks. She kept a keen and wary eye upon all the children, not forgetting an occasional glance at the 'old man' in the doorway.

"She saw me as I came up, and from her look I thought she was of the opinion that I intended to interfere. Advancing to the doorway, and roughly pushing her husband aside, she demanded my business.

" 'Nothing, madame,' I answered as gently as possible; 'I merely dropped in as I came along to see how things were going.'

" 'Well, you needn't wait,' was the reply in an irritated way, 'there's trouble here, an' lots of it, too, but I kin manage my own affairs without the help of outsiders. This is jest a family row, but I'll teach these brats their places ef I hev to lick the hide off ev'ry one of them. I don't do much talkin', but I run this house, an' I don't want no one sneakin' 'round tryin' to find out how I do it, either.'

"That's the case here with us," the President said in conclusion. "We must let the other nations know that we propose to settle our family row in our own way, and 'teach these brats their places' (the seceding States) if we have to 'lick the hide off' of each and every one of them. And, like the old woman, we don't want any 'sneakin' 'round' by other countries who would like to find out how we are to do it, either."

Once Mr. Lincoln was riding horseback. He came to an overturned load of hay. The boy driving the team was quite "upset," and striving hard to right the load. Lincoln asked the boy to a farmhouse with him where he could get some help. After much persuasion the boy consented, and after lunch he said: "Dad won't like my being away so long," and started back to his load of hay. Lincoln said: "Don't hurry; I'll send some help back to aid you." The lad replied: "Don't you know that dad's under the hay?"

A lawyer, opposed to Lincoln, was trying to convince a jury that precedent was superior to law, and that custom made things legal in all cases. Lincoln rose to answer him. He told the jury he would argue the case in the same way. He said: "Old 'Squire Bagly, from Menard, came into my office and said, 'Lincoln, I want your advice as a lawyer. Has a man what's been elected a justice of the peace a right to issue a marriage license?' I told him he had not; when the old 'squire threw himself back in his chair very indignantly, and said, 'Lincoln, I thought you was a lawyer. Now, Bob Thomas and me had a bet on this thing, and we agreed to let you decide; but, if this is your opinion, I don't want it, for I know a thunderin' sight better, for I have been 'squire now for eight years and have done it all the time.' "

They say that Mr. Lincoln was never so happy as when some of his old chums from Illinois with whom he had sat around the cabins there in Illinois, swapping stories in his early days, came to Washington. He was delighted to see them. He used to invite them to the White House and have them swap stories about the old periods, and such newer ones as would come to him in the later period. As this particular gentleman was about to leave he said to Mr. Lincoln, "I want you to be honest with me. How do you like being president of the United States?" Well, Mr. Lincoln smiled and looked at him and then said, "You have heard the story, haven't you, about the man as he was ridden out of town on a rail, tarred and feathered, somebody asked him how he liked it, and his reply was if it was not for the honor of the thing, he would much rather walk."

The President told of a Southern Illinois preacher who, in the course of his sermon at a rural church, asserted that the

Saviour was the only perfect man who had ever appeared in this world; also, that there was no record in the Bible, or elsewhere, of any perfect woman having lived on earth. Whereupon there arose in the rear of the church a persecuted-looking personage who, the parson having stopped speaking, said: 'I know a perfect woman, and I've heard of her about every day for the last six years,' 'Who was she?' asked the minister. 'My husband's first wife,' replied the afflicted female."

President Lincoln, during a discussion on other matters, relieved tension by telling two stories about applications for two inventions to control poultry:

The first device, called a "hen walker," was intended to prevent hens from scratching up the garden, and consisted of a movable brace attached to the hen's legs so that at each scratch the hen was propelled forward, and so by successive scratches all the way out of the garden. The other device was called a "double-back-action hen persuader," which was so adjusted under the hen's nest that as each egg was laid it fell through a trap door out of sight of the author, who would then be persuaded to lay another egg.

On another occasion Mr. Lincoln said that the claim that the Mexican War was not aggressive reminded him of the farmer who asserted, "I ain't greedy 'bout land, I only just wants what jines mine."

Then there were the stories in which subjects considered either too sacred or too profane were introduced. One described a rough frontier cabin, with children running wild, and a hard-worked wife and mother, slatternly and unkempt, not overhappy perhaps, but with a woman's loyal instinct to make the best of things before a stranger. Into this setting strode an itinerant Methodist, unctious and insistent, selling Bibles as well as preaching salvation. She received him with frontier hospitality, but grew restive under questioning she deemed intrusive and finally answered rather sharply that of course they owned a Bible. He challenged her to produce it. A search revealed nothing. The children were called to her aid, and at last one of them unearthed and held up for inspection a few tattered leaves. Protest and reproaches on the part of the visitor, but on her own stanch sticking to her colors. "She had no idea," she declared, "that they were so nearly out of the Bible."

Artemus Ward, the most popular Civil War humorist, once stated that Lincoln said that his father was an artist true to life, for he made a scarecrow so artfully bad that the frightened crows brought back the corn they had stolen two years before.

Ward also told U.S. Supreme Court Justice, Salmon P. Chase, that his father was an artist who was true to life, for he made a scarecrow so bad that the crows brought back the corn they had stolen two years before.

One of his personal guards recalled the President told this story:

This was at the Soldier's Home, when one of the boys, speaking for the Company and encouraged by Mr. Lincoln's evident interest in their welfare, expressed the belief that the Company was of no use there and was needed at the front. Mr. Lincoln prefaced a kindly admonition as to a soldier's duty to obey orders without question, by saying: "You boys remind me of a farmer friend of mine in Illinois, who said he could never understand why the Lord put the curl in a pig's tail. It never seemed to him to be either useful or ornamental, but he reckoned that the Almighty knew what he was doing when he put it there. I don't think I need guards, but Mr. Stanton, Secretary of War, thinks I do, and as it is in his Department, if you go to the front he will insist upon others coming from the front to take your place." Then he added, with a twinkle in his eye— "And boys, I reckon it is pleasanter and safer here than there."

Major General John Cochrane recalled an illustration with which President Lincoln characterized the fatal facility of the Rapahannock transit, when he subsequently described to him the particulars [of the defeat at Fredericksburg].

"Well," he said, "I thought the case was suspicious. It reminded me of a young acquaintance out in Illinois, who, having secured the affections of a lass, was proceeding to her father for his permission to marry her, when he saw him plowing in a field.

" 'Hallo,' cried the impatient youth, 'I want your darter.'

" 'Take her,' said the old man as, without turning, he trudged after the plow.

" 'A little too easy,' exclaimed the prudent swain, scratching his head, 'a little too darned easy.' "

———

Mr. Lincoln gave the following account of the first announcement of the Emancipation Proclamation in a Cabinet meeting.

He read it through, and there was a dead silence. Presently Mr. Chase spoke. He said he liked all but so and so, instancing a clause; then someone else made an objection, and then another, until all had said something. Then the President said: "Gentlemen, this reminds me of the story of the man who had been away from home, and when he was coming back was met by one of his farm hands, who greeted him after his fashion: 'Master, the little pigs are dead, and the old sow's dead, too, but I didn't like to tell you all at once.' "

———

To illustrate a shifting political policy, Lincoln told of a farm boy whose father instructed him in plowing a new furrow. "Steer for that yoke of oxen standing at the further end of the field." The father went away. The boy followed instructions. But the oxen began moving. The boy followed them around the field, furrowed a circle instead of a line!

———

One story James M. Scovel said Lincoln told to illustrate

the petty jealousies and bickerings among Congressmen and army generals. Lincoln was reminded of two Illinois men, one Farmer Jones, a churchman gifted in prayer, the other Fiddler Simpkins, welcome at every country merrymaking. At one Wednesday evening prayer meeting Brother Jones made a wonderful prayer which touched the hearts of all. And Brother Simpkins felt called on to rise and say, "Brethring and sistring, I know that I can't make half as good a prayer as Brother Jones, but by the grace of God I *can* fiddle the shirt off of him."

Mr. Lincoln was discussing the relative merits of New England rum and corn juice, as he called it, to illuminate the human mind, he told this story of John Moore, who resided south of Blooming Grove, and subsequently became state treasurer:

Mr. Moore came to Bloomington one Saturday in a cart drawn by a fine pair of red steers. For some reason he was a little late starting home, and besides his brown jug, he otherwise had a good load on. In passing through the grove that night, one wheel of his cart struck a stump or root and threw the pole out of the ring of the yoke. The steers, finding themselves free, ran away, and left John Moore sound asleep in his cart, where he remained all night. Early in the morning, he roused himself, and looking over the side of the cart and around in the woods, he said: "If my name is John Moore, I've lost a pair of steers; if my name ain't John Moore, I've found a cart."

Often he told stories, and cracked jokes, for the sheer fun of it. Once he was looking idly out of the window of his Springfield law office at the muddy, rain-soaked street below. Along came a proud lady wearing a many-plumed hat, and in picking her was carefully, she slipped and fell.

"Reminds me of a duck," said Lincoln to a companion.

"Why is that?"

"Feathers on her head and down on her behind!"

Lincoln sent General Hooker to take over the Army; Hooker rushed into action, sending his dispatches with his heading: "Headquarters in the saddle." Grinning, Lincoln said: "The trouble with Hooker is that he's got his headquarters where his hindquarters ought to be."

An Illinois man who had known John Hay from boyhood, was expressing to Uncle Abe, after the massacre at Olustee [20 February 1864], some regret that he should have supposed him capable of any military position.

"About Hay," said Uncle Abe, "that fact was, I was pretty much like Jim Hawks, out in Illinois, who sold a dog to a hunting neighbor, as a first-rate coon dog. A few days after, the fellow brought him back, saying he 'wasn't worth a cuss for coons.' 'Well,' said Jim, 'I tried him for everything else, and he wasn't worth a d——n, and so I thought he must be good for coons.' "

Lawrence Weldon, a friend from circuit-riding days, told of this tale: "Do you remember a story," Mr. Lincoln asked, "that Bob [Lewis] used to tell us about his going to Missouri to look up some Mormon lands that belong to his father?" I said: "Mr President, I have forgotten the details of that story, and I wish you would tell it." He then said that when Robert became of age he found among the papers of his father's a number of warrants and patents for lands in North-east Missouri, and he concluded the best thing he could do was to go to Missouri and investigate the condition of things. It being before the days of the railroads, he started on horseback with a pair of old-fashioned saddle-bags. When he arrived where he supposed his land was situated, he stopped, hitched his horse, and went into a cabin standing close by the roadside. He found the proprietor, a lean, lanky, leathery-looking man, engaged in the pioneer business of making bullets preparatory to a hunt. Mr. Lewis observed, on entering, a rifle suspended on a couple of buck horns above the fire. He said to the man: "I am looking up some lands that I think belong to my father," and inquired of the man in what section he lived. Without having ascertained the section, Mr. Lewis proceeded to exhibit his title papers in evidence, and having established a good title as he thought, said to the man: "Now, that is my title, what is yours?" The pioneer, who had by this time become somewhat interested in the proceeding, pointed his long finger toward the rifle, and said: "Young man, do you see that gun?" Mr. Lewis frankly admitted that he did. "Well," said he, "that is my title, and if you don't get out of here pretty damned quick you will feel the force of it." Mr. Lewis hurriedly put his title papers in his saddle-bags, mounted his pony, and galloped down the road, and, as Bob says, the old pioneer snapped his gun twice at him before he could turn the corner. Lewis said that he had never been back to disturb that man's title since. "Now," said Mr. Lincoln, "the military authorities have the same title against the civil authorities that closed out Bob's Mormon title in Missouri."

Perhaps the best way to conclude this section of Abraham Lincoln's funny stories, is to relate a lovely and revealing tale illustrating the importance of humor in his life—the joy and fun it expressed; the sadness and pain it concealed.

Two Quaker ladies were traveling on the railroad, and were heard discussing the probable termination of the war. "I think," said the first, "that Jefferson will succeed." "Why does thee think so?" asked the other. "Because Jefferson is a praying man." "And so is Abraham a praying man," objected the second. "Yes, but the Lord will think Abraham is joking," the first replied, conclusively.

"The tractor repair shop in town gave me this loaner . . ."

"We got tired of waiting for vandals to do it . . . so we shot it ourselves."

Section 3

Early Farm and Ranch Humor

"It looks good, but it sounds funny."

"My next number is one I wrote myself—one that clarifies the role of each creature, great and small, in the preservation of the American family farm system."

"Harley, ol' boy, we're presenting you with a nice watch and putting you out to pasture!"

Introduction

These wonderfully funny stories, jokes and poems are from the 1920's, selected from FARM LIFE and other farm magazines. This magazine was enormously popular having national circulation of 2,000,000 copies a month. It was published in Spencer, Indiana.

FARM LIFE featured "essas" by Abe Martin, the most popular country comic of that day. Born in Indiana, Abe Martin reflected the dirt farmers' opinion and did, in fact, help largely in the formation of them. In his day, he was to farm families what Mike Royko today is for city folks. But Abe Martin leaned lightly on satire.

The cute, phonetic spelling of Ben Puttin-it-off takes a little practice. But once you get used to words spelled the way they sound, and you read/listen as if the words were spoken, then you'll have a great time with old Ben who procrastinates (Ben Puttin-it-off!) just as we all do.

These stories, jokes and essays reinforce the view that if we are to look wisely at life today on the farm or ranch, we must put it in perspective—the broad view. And the humor of earlier times helps us achieve a more balanced look at our lives. We gain a feeling of kinship, of familiarity with the ranchers and farmers who worked the land and livestock ahead of us. The jokes and funny stories they told about bankers, preachers, wives, kids, crops, livestock and weather are as relevant and funny today as then. And 100 years from now farmers and ranchers will find them just as funny—and relevant.

Here are the jokes and funny stories that tickled Grandpa and Grandma, as well as *their* Pa and Ma. And now YOU!

"My feet are killing me."

Here's Some Tall Corn Evidence

Dear Sirs:—I see that Mr. Smith of Illinois and Mr. McMillion and James Auten are telling about their large corn stalks and what they use them for. Also Mr. Walter Durnell, Kentucky, has mentioned the big corn they used to raise in Missouri.

Now, as I am a Missourian, I can vouch for Mr. Durnell. But we don't fool away our time and waste our stalks like these other fellows do. We decided several years ago that silos were a mighty good investment, and as the corn stalks were so much cheaper than wood, and better too, we use the stalks for our silos.

We cut them at the joints and get about sixteen twenty-foot silos from an ordinary stalk. We saw off the ears and usually get from three to five silos full from each stalk.

We only use our popcorn stalks for such as bridge piling, roads, telegraph poles and fence posts. —Chas. M. Mc-Dowell, Mo.

Talk about your tall corn, give me your ear, or both of them, while I tell you about some corn that I grew in Missouri. To get the seed I crossed some Tom Thumb pop corn with the ordinary corn used here, which will make good sized saw logs. The first day of May, I planted one grain. Next morning I had forgotten the planted grain, but I did wonder when I had set that telephone pole in the middle of the garden. When I examined it a little later much to my surprise it had doubled in girth and height.

Not till then did I remember planting the one grain of corn. I felt mighty proud of my plant-breeding venture, so when my brother came over that evening, riding his saddle horse, I opened the garden gate and asked him to look at my corn. He rode up to it, looked at it a while, and became so befuddled that he tied his horse to the stalk and ran to the house. I was only shortly behind him.

After collecting our scattered wits we returned to the scene, and the horse was nowhere in sight. Then my brother looked up into the corn stalks, and gave a gurgling exclamation. I looked up, and saw the horse hanging by his reins full a hundred feet high and rising higher every minute. I ran for an axe and tried to cut the mighty stalk down, but it was growing so fast that I could not hit twice in the same place. Finally the stalk jerked the axe out of my hand.

Some one advised me to try corn borers in an effort to kill the stalk. I laughed at this, but was persuaded to import some from Ohio. I placed them on the ground, and recognizing their prey, they dug down to the roots and commenced the work of destruction. Soon the stalk stopped growing and then died. My next problem was to get rid of the borers. I set fire to the stalk, and it produced so much heat that we had only a mild winter that year.

When the borers destroyed so colossal a giant, think what they do to just the small fifteen feet corn that all the states except Missouri raise.

No, I haven't any seed because of course, the giant was killed before it was ripe and I burned the seed left as I did not want so much confusion around me again. —Joseph L. Love, Mo.

P. S. —Next time, I will tell you how I harvest corn at the Rodeo. —J. L. L.

P. P. S. —That is, if that corn stalk doesn't sucker. —J. L. L.

To the Editors:—A man who was driving 3,000 head of 1,000-pound cattle from Texas to Abilene, Kansas, came to a swollen river, that he could not cross; hoping to find a suitable crossing he went up the river and saw a tree blown down across it. The tree was hollow. He drove the cattle through this, and 3,000 went in, but only 2,700 came out on the other side. Looking through he could see no cattle. But following the cattle through, he found the 300 in a hollow limb. —O. W. Stephens, Ind.

Dear Editors: Out here in the early days, it was so dry none of the corn that was planted would come up. Farmers were ready to quit planting corn. Then one farmer who was changing a corral fence to take in part of his would-be cornfield, dis-covered in one of the post holes that his corn had been grow-ing downward.

Investigation revealed that the climate being so dry, the corn could not come up, and so went down. Farmers at once started shucking their corn with spades. As a result of seed improvement corn was grown that reached depths unheard of. Many underground rivers were discovered in the course of the harvests.

Later, irrigation wells were installed, and this variety of corn was abandoned for the more convenient surface variety. Thus another art was lost to the world. —Otis Harkness, Kans.

Dear Editors: Last year I visited my uncle down in Iowa. Of course he raises corn—wowee-ee! It sure was corn! It grew so fast he had to have two men stationed at each stalk to chop off the ears as they went by. One day a fellow missed an ear and it caught under his belt. By Heck, you won't believe it, but it carried him up so far that we had to shoot dog biscuits up to him with a blunderbuss to keep the poor fellow from starving. Yours till the horseflies, Harry Ekdahl, Minn.

Dear Editors: How many of the tall corn growers ever heard of a corn tree that grows here in Pennsylvania? This corn is not planted annually, for it continues to grow from one gener-ation to another. Some specimens are a century old and tower high in the air and are thrifty yet. We have one in our yard that is probably fifty feet high, and measures eleven feet in circumference.

When the corn is ripe it drops to the ground from a height of 30 to 45 feet, and you need only pick up the kernels. Folks have gathered two bushels or more from one plant. The ker-nels are too large for domestic fowl to eat, but hogs relish them exceedingly.

This kind of tree makes lumber which is used wherever durable, lasting wood is needed, such as in buildings and ships. Juice extracted from the bark is used to tan leather. There is hardly any waste in the tree. Even the ashes make lye and the lye is made into soap.

Now this corn story is the truth packed in a nutshell. But I wonder why the yield of other nut bearing trees is named from the trees such as chestnuts, beachnut and hickory nut, while that of the oak is called an acorn? —R. E. S., Pa.

———————

Dear Sirs: Let me tell you about when I was in the bee business along the sand dunes of western Michigan. The bees worked hard, yet took all summer to fill a hive. At that time English sparrows had become very thick, and it seemed not to have a thing to do. So I crossed them with my bees.

Well, you ought to see the result. They loaded themselves so heavy they could not fly, and had to walk back to the hive. I fixed a hook under each wing, and hung a one-pound section on each side, and then things commenced to happen. They filled all my hives and all I could beg, borrow or steal— this the first day. That night they commenced to bore holes in the sand dunes with their stingers. By fall the whole country was filled with honey, and when it froze hard enough I took a pair of ice tongs and pulled the comb out of the sand dunes, and hauled them to town. You probably remember the year when honey took a slump and everything was all stuck up.

Those sparrow bees are all dead now, but the effects of their work are still evident. The beeswax ran all over the state, and plastered down the mortgages so tight no one can raise them. —A. J. Walter, Mich.

———————

Tall Corn in Kansas

To the Editors: —I see by your February number that Mr. Smith of Illinois has raised some tall corn stalks, but seems to be shy of telling their height. Now I have the honor of raising two of the tallest stalks of corn ever raised in Kansas and am jealous of other states with their claims. And they will have to show me, for I can furnish affidavits for the truth of my statements.

The shortest stalk, from the ground to the ear, was 37 feet and 10 inches and to tassel, 40 feet and 8 inches. Rather long fishing poles, but you could cut them down to suit. —T. C. Johnson, Kansas

P. S. I don't want you to think I am a liar, for every word in the above is the truth. Five years ago I did not empty my silos and there were two stalks of corn that grew out of the silage and up over the top of the silos. You will note that I say from the ground to the ear. T. C. J.

And corn isn't the only crop that creates liars out of honest, wholesome, truthful farmers. In Indiana, they stretch the blanket over some big feet. Witness this:

Milt Slemmons on Big Feet
by Herman Fetzer

"I presume" said Milt Slemmons, unburdening his shoulder of a sackful of newly-sharpened plow-points, "that you have never heard the story of Zebulon Thistlepoof. He was before your time. He had the biggest feet that I have ever seen or want to see. It was an inspiring sight to see him walk down the main street to Kerriston when I was young.

"Many's the time I have seen him shelter little children from the rain by standing on his head and spreading his feet over them like a sheep shed. He used to pull out his corns with a stump-puller and trim his toe nails with a scythe.

"Long about nine o'clock any morning you'd see a couple of long, black objects protruding around the corner and into the postoffice, and ten minutes later Zebulon would follow his shoes into the store. He couldn't get around a narrow corner. He had to lie down, lay his feet into the corner at right angles, turn on his side and get up that way.

"He had a soft heart. Once when a boat load of young people fell into the mill race he took off his shoe and threw it in and they clumb into it and rowed ashore. Only one young fellow was missing and it's still a question whether he was drowned or whether he was still in the shoe when Zebulon put it back on. It was the only time Zeb ever took off his shoe from the time he was of age.

"But Zeb went an got liquored up one time and laid out in the corn field all night. While he slept, three billposters from Fort Wayne came along and nailed a big sign across both feet so he couldn't get up. The nails they had drove in gave him blood poison and he died while they were pulling them out of his feet. The billposters sued his estate for $37.50 destruction of property and won it."

Dear Editor: I have been reading about your large corn. I don't need to fotygraf but I'm known as truthful Dan. First off, we can't find any use for our corn stalks because our cotton stems furnish us telephone poles, fence posts, lumber, etc. But yore readers might like to know that we made ten loads of firewood out of our corn stalks. D.H. Glass, Texas.

The Tall Corn Still Towers
*But Some Are Doubting Whether
Everyone is Sticking Close to Facts*

In Defense of Truth Dear

Editor: —I joined the Ananias Corn Club in order to modify downright falsehoods, thinking at the time that other writers might pattern after me and thus preserve truth. But alas, my labor of love was lost! All the writers have grown utterly reckless in their statements. Everyone knows it is bad to tell a whopper like Smith did, and then tell a worse one to maintain it. And it's still worse for Mr. Johnson of Kansas, to study all night on a story to sustain Mr. Smith.

Few have ever come to my defense through life. Oh, well, it is known that a good fruit tree is always full of clubs. Mr. Johnson has not clubbed me but a Lady Writer of Kansas has. So I declare war on Kansas. I regret this state of affairs, as Missouri borders on that state. They should be sister states. Oh woman, ye have not transgressed against a Kentuckian, but a Missourian. Shall the battle be to the finish, or will you lift the white flag? Believe me, not all the houses in Missouri are built of logs and rough lumber. The Lady evidently saw such houses on or near the Kansas border.

The time we raised our corn there was long after John Brown. And there is no telling what would have been the possible evolution of that corn, had not the sunflower state caused us to sell out and more away. Two great evils came from Kansas—cyclones and grasshoppers. About the time we thought we had corn developed fairly well, the freight cars would come through laden with grasshoppers ten inches long, and every mother's son of them was impudent enough to spit tobacco juice at a luckless on-looker. The grasshoppers almost destroyed all green crops. Some good Missourian speak up and say that this was true, along about '73 or '74.

Another evil beginning in Kansas, was a burn-up year and a drown-out year. Then, along came one of those Kansas-born cyclones and literally blew what we had left to kingdom come. We barely escaped with our lives. Yours for the safeguarding of truth. —Walter L. Durnell, Ky.

Iowa Speaks Up

Editors Farm Life: Here in Iowa the tourists are obliged to turn their lights on in the day time, as the corn on each side of the road is like going through a tunnel. We have trained our corn so the leaves and ears grow up and down the highway so they will not block traffic. Ears are trained to grow about a foot apart and when we husk we climb to the top and pick as we come down. We used the giant stalks to stretch fence wire on one year, driving the staples into the stalks. But it gave the corn a disagreeable rusty favor. —Lee Love, Iowa.

Editors Farm Life: I have been reading the big corn stalk stories—lies I calls 'em—in Farm Life, and am wondering if this Smith who seems to be the bell wether, is the John Smith I once knew down in Missouri.

There are a great many Smiths in Missouri. Once at a big Democrat rally down there, a telegram came for Mr. Smith. The chairman asked if there was any one named Smith in the audience, and 200 stood up. He announced that this telegram was addressed to John Smith; 96 of the 200 sat down.

I live now way out in New Mexico, where corn is not grown for house legs, as two or three pine trees cut into suitable lengths makes a house pattern. But oh my, such yields of corn! We use seed taken from the old Aztec ruins which abound here, and I hesitate to tell the truth about it as I know it will be hard to believe.

This corn, taken from the old ruins, keep that in mind, if planted near any other vegetable just seems to swallow it up. The yield is so great that farmers do not count by bushels, but by car loads per acre.

One of my neighbors, Jim Nubbin by name, told me he once planted some of this corn near a hedge fence, and was greatly surprised when autumn come to find many good ears of corn hanging from the bodark limbs that hung close to a stalk of corn.

Jim is a good man, calls the preacher brother, says grace at the table, and all that, yet I never have been able to swallow all this tale at one time, without taking more salt than was good for my digestion.

Nevertheless, this Aztec corn is so prolific, that it is almost impossible to plant few enough grains in the hill, as one grain in a hill produces such a profusion of stalks that the thinning out constitutes the bigger part of the cultivation.

Nubbin says for several years he has planted only one grain to the hill but finds this too much for his black valley land, and hereafter he expects to plant fewer until he gets the proper number to bring best results.

To be frank with you, Mr. Editor, I very much doubt the truth of these corn stalk yarns told by Smith, Johnson, McMillion et al, and cannot understand why these one hundred per cent Americans should thus slander the holy cause of agriculture. Yours for truth. —T. P. Maddox, N. Mex.

———————

Dear Editors: Corn grows so fast down here that when we drop a grain we have to jump out of the way to keep the up-shooting blades from knocking us down. We go down a row planting the corn and come back gathering it. The ears grow so large that we have to load them on flat cars with steam loaders.

Corn weevils grow so big here in Louisiana that we have to go in the crib and shoot them with buckshot. We have to use plows made all of iron, because wood will grow limbs instantly on our rich soil. I left my ax sticking in the ground over night. The handle was made of hickory, and when I awake next morning it had grown up and was loaded with hickory nuts. Peanuts grow so large here that we shell them and use the hulls to make fishing boats. Yours for more and better corn. — Kendreth Parker, La.

Some elegant poetry by early farm and ranch esthetes (egg heads?).

"DOWN WHERE THE VEST BEGINS"

Down where the belt-clasp's a little stronger,
Down where the pants should be an inch longer,
    That's where the vest begins.

Down where you wish you were a bit slighter,
Where the shirt that shows is a little lighter,
Where each day the buttons grow tighter,
    That's where the vest begins.

Down where the pains are in the making,
Where each heavy meal will soon start aching,
    That's where the vest begins.

Where each added pound is the cause of sighing,
When you know in your heart that the scales aren't lying,
And you just have to guess when your shoes need tying,—
    Well,—That's where the vest begins.

—Helen Crenshaw.

Lots of people get fat without broadenin' themselves.

Here lie the bones
  Of Wilbur Wump
Who drove too fast
  And hit a bump.
And left the road,
  'Ere he could jump,
And wrapped his car
  Around a stump.
Remains are at the city dump—
  The car—not Wump.

_____

A chewing gum girl
A cud-chewing cow,
They're both alike
'Tho different somehow.
Oh yes, I see it all now,
It's the thoughtful look
on the face of the cow.

_____

ON THE ART OF STORY-TELLING

Listen, feller, what are we to do with or to the bird who firmly believes he can tell a story when that is the one thing he can probably do a good many things but?

A dumbell who would more or less cheerfully admit his inability to connect up the plumbing, draw a cartoon, write a poem, grind valves, repair a watch without having any wheels left over, convince his wife of something she doubted, walk a slack wire, juggle three baseballs and a water-pitcher, sing soprano, spell Central American mountain names, extract cube root without looking at the rules, or any other difficult thing, cannot be convinced in any way that story-telling is the poorest thing he is at.

He will start the story in the middle, stop and correct himself. Or begin with the point of it and build it up from there, now and then going back to say "No, I'm getting ahead of my story—it wasn't his brother, it was his father—yes, that was— no, it was his brother after all."

Then he will begin again, stop and study and muse over it

and finally laugh heartily and tell it leaving out the point and expecting you to laugh also.

Some time when a rightful denizen of the boobyhatch or the cuckoory or the mental hoosegow buttonholes me with a yarn a thousand and ten years old and butchers it in my presence at the expense of fifteen minutes of my time—some time, I say, when some such bimbo assails me and commits this sort of crime, I shall bust him one where it will do the most good—not on the head, for that wouldn't stop anything, but on the mouth, where his entire activity takes place.

———————

. . . Hank Scofield takes his misfortunes like a man— he blames them all on his wife.

———————

"Go, my son, and shut that shutter,"
A mother to her son did utter,
"The shutter's shut," the son did mutter,
"And I can't shut it any shutter."

———————

Mabel bought a bathing suit,
It was pretty beyond a doubt,
But when she climbed inside it,
The most of her stayed out.

———————

Oh, the Chigger ain't no bigger
Than the point of a pin,
But the bump that he raises,
It itches like the blazes,
And that's where the rub comes in!

———————

The Troubles of
Poor Ben Puttin-It-Off

His Sin Finds Him Out

Deer Editr —I just got throo my Noo Yeers rezzylootn, and thay start thisaway:

"I solmly xpekt 2 leev hoam an stay away frum saim enny aw evry time Marthy haz Preechr Weeks hear fr dinnr."

I riz at 5 a.m. this Sundy mornin, aided konsidrbl by Kompulshn (uthrwize naimd Marthy) as nevr had a peasfl minit til Bruthr Meeks tin henry went clattrn doun the rode.

I wair jest like wunna them bais ignobl slavs the poick tels about.

I trukld doun sellr an fetcht pikiz an plum prsurvz an kand peetchz, gettn the rong thing moast evr time an havn to go bak.

An I tuk out ashz an swep the frunt poartch, an put the xtry leef in the taibl.

I toatd wood to the parir heetr an the kook stoav, tern an tern about, an I drawd wattr enuff to flote a steembote.

I mopt the kitchn twiste, the ferst time not bein sadisfacktry to the preesidn ossifr.

An I eavn tide a naiprn around me an startd to set the taibl, but when I dropt a dish o buttr I wair xkoozd frum this dooty.

An the, to add to the visissytoodz uv life I had to shaiv an put on a kleen shert and shaik hanz with Bruthr an Sistr Meeks, and be kalld Bruthr Putinoff."

Besides, I had to set at the hed uv the taibl an pass thingz, an wair my best mannrz, whitch wairnt enny 2 fansy, jedjn frum Marthyz ibrow wireless an undr taibl footwerk.

Bfuthr Meeks appollyjizd fer havn to "eet an run," bekawz he had to preech a fewnrl that aftrnoon.

"We doant keer at all," sezzi. "Enny time yoo get ready to leave, wy jest pike out."

I doant see enny thing rong in that polite remark, but Marthy pootni lookt a hoal in my Sundy kote.

Dinner beein oavr, Marthy fetcht the Bible, an the Preechr sez:

"What shall I reed?"

"Ennything, so its short," sezzi. He lookt at me kwair like an went to ternin the leevz reel fast.

Jest then my plain kards begin rattln outa the book unto the floar, as a silents thik enuff to slise fell oavr the party.

Bruthr Meeks peard oavr hiz specks at the kards, an then at me.

Sistr Meeks kleard her throat an glaird at me, and pattd Marthyz hand with deep simpathy.

An Marthy, wel she ternd white an red, and maybe bloo, an I kood pootni heer her grindn her stoar teeth in raij.

"Well, well," I chirpt, fealn that sumboddy otta say sumthn, "I wundr hoo put them implymnts uv saitn thair?"

Noboddy seamed to no, so I slithrd out to the korn krib.

Wairnt that jest my luk to frget to talk them kardz out aftr the gaim me an Sam Slackman had the nite afore. Mathy had kum hoam onxpected, an we had hid em in the book.

Whad Marthy say?

What I tel her?

That, az the fellr sez, is anuthr stoary.

Yoarz fr a happy Noo Yeer.

BEN PUTTIN-IT-OFF

She's let her figure run amuck—
    Has cast her shape adrift.
In fighting fat she's had no luck;
    She'd be a pill to lift.
Her school-girl color is no more;
    She puts no make-up on.
She's bought no tresses from the store,
    Though most of hers are gone.
The hats she wears are perfect frights;
    Her shoes low-heeled and wide.
Were one to see that same in tights,
    One should be horrified.
Her chins are numerous and large;
    Her ankles out of plumb.
If street cars made pro rata charge,
    I guess she couldn't come.

She plays not auction nor mah jongg—
    "Five hundred" is her speed.
She does not dance or lilt a song—

These tricks she does not need.
Nay, through in heft she is immense,
    A total loss in looks,
Men speak her name in reverence,
    For, lordy, how she cooks!

. . . When you have anythin' to say to a mule, allus say it to his face.
(It pays to be upfront with some critters.)

Two ladies met a boy one day;
    His legs were briar scratched,
His clothes were blue, but a nut-brown hue
    Marked the seat where his pants were patched.
They bubbled with joy at the blue-clad boy,
    With his spot of nut-brown hue.
"Why didn't you patch with a color to match?"
    They chuckled: "Why not in blue?
Come don't be coy, my blue-brown boy,
    Speak out," and they laughed with glee.
And he blushed rose red while he bashfully said:
    "That ain't no patch, that's me."

. . . Some pleasantry was indulged in on Main Street yes-tiddy when Old Uncle Neb was gettin' ready to leave town with his wife in their buggy. When she started to climb in the buggy alone, she remarked, "Neb you ain't so gal-alnt as you wuz when you wuz a boy." And Neb replied, "Mandy, you ain't so boy-yant as you wuz when you wuz a gal."

And Still More Tall Corn

Dear Editor: —In the June issue I notice that Walter L. Durnell raised some fine corn back in Missouri in his boyhood days—said no country but Missouri could equal it.
I raised a very good stalk of corn in Old Kent once.

I wintered 40 head of cattle, 60 head of sheep on the fodder off that stalk. It had two ears, one small ear which I ground into corn meal. I sold 60 bushels of meal from that ear. The other one was larger. It took a good pair of mules to pull the grains off the cob. The cob I hewed off at both ends, dug the pith out of the center, raised it, covered it with galvanized roofing, and I know I have the best silo in the United States.

I won't tell you how large the stalk was for I hate to make those guys ashamed of the small stalks they have raised. That was about the best stalk I have raised. But I am getting old—I can't raise corn like I used to. —Thomas Kinslow, Ky.

Editors Farm Life: I notice in your paper where some of your readers have been giving their experience in raising corn. It reads to me like they have been raising pop corn. I raised corn myself a few years ago, which grew so fast that when squirrels tried to climb to the ears they would starve to death before they got there. The game commissioner stopped me from growing it, on account of destroying game, and the Humane Society, for cruelty to dumb animals.

I did not build any barns out of the logs, but I hollowed out the cobs and used them for small buildings, such as cow stables, chicken houses, and to put winter fruit and potatoes in. I still have a few kernels stacked out and will sell them: one apiece for $4.00 per hundred, buyers to pay the freight. But understand I will not cut a kernel for any man. - R. V. S., W. Va.

. . . The Parson sez he don't mind folks in the congregation pullin' out their watches on him, but it gets his goat when they put 'em up to their ear to see if they're goin'.

. . . When you think your settin' in clover, dont fergit about the bees.

The Troubles of
Poor Ben Puttin-It-Off

Martha Meets Disaster

Deer Editr —Foaz that think Friday iz unluky hav gotta nuthr think kumn. Mundy iz the hoodoo da fr the huzbn hooz wife duz the famly washng.

"I'm telln yoo wunst agen," sez my Sunshine Sweatness, last Mundy, "that my kloaze line iz saggn terbl, an I wanchoo to ty it up hier."

"Joo think, woomn," sezzi, "that I ken leeve my bizness too pottr awl day around yoar littl affairz. I've alreddy drord nine barls uv wattr an fecht in a wagon load uv wood. Ime woar out."

"Ime afeard yoo air exawstd," snears Marthy, stackn the brekfst dishes snappily, "but I want that line fixt b4 yoo xpire, ennyway."

"This step laddr iz on the back poartch," sezzi, slammn the kitchn doar an herryin to the barn.

It wair, mayby, haffn our laitr when I herd a wild kawl frm the hous.

"Hollr awl yoo pleez," sezzi, goin on with my work. "I ainta kumn.

But sumthn in Marthy's voise, "Ben, O Ben," maid me fling away my whittln stik an gallop toarj the alarm.

Throo the barn lot an aroun the hous, an down the yard I went, an in the far kornr uv the yard I see a fearsm site.

Marthy wair hangn herseff by her hanz on the lim uv the sweat appl trea, danglin her kongress gaitrs with hoalz in the toaz, plum sicks feet frum the groun. An her tippn the skailz at ny 200!

Belo her, on the groun, the bustd remainz uv the step laddr explaind it awl. She had klum up to fix that line, an the laddr had gon blooey.

"Herry, Ben, and get me down," she sreax. "An it aint funny; neathr," she adz, fewrsly.

"Well, well," sezzi, snickrn a littl in spite uv her sad predickymnt. She did look amoozn, her bein so fatn an awl, an swingn up thair in her wash day kostoom—bloo kalikr, wunna my oald koats and red shaul oavr her hed an sidewaize akrost wun i.

"Joo rekn," sezzi, ketchn hoald uv her ankls, "that yookd jump fide hoaldyr feat?"

"Uv awl the big idjts, yoor the prize winnr," sez she, kickn so vilntly that I let loos and backt away.

"Maybe," sezzi, "that I kood hold wunna them boards soze yoo kood slide down it, an—howdjoo kum to be up thair, enny way? I wair aimn to ficks that line, but I jest kep puttn it off—"

"Didn't kum to be up hear," she gasps. "Kum—to—ficks—line—fetch fethr bed—put belo—moov laddr."

"Must I fetch the kuvvrs, too?" sezzi, realizn how perticklr she iz about her bed kuvvrs. She woant eavn let Ebeneazr the pup up thair fr a nap.

"Moove laddr—kwik," she gasps, an I got it away jest a split secknd b4 my ducky duv kaim tumbin to the groun.

She groand and tuk on konsidraibl, but I toaldr sheed autop beglad she wair abl to finish the washn the secknd day aftrwrds, stedda havn 2 hiar sumboddy to doo it.

She wairnt really hert a bit—jest skind up her elboaz an broozd boath neaz and maid a bloo brooz on her forrid an a grean wun onr jaw an rencht her back a littl.

The brooz on hr jaw wair externl, an had no effeck on the aktivity uv the saim, as I diskivvrd to my sorro.

I wair to blaim, akkordn to my akyoozr, bekawz:

1.—I put off byin a noo step laddr.

2.—I put off mendn the oald wun.

3.—I put off tyin up the line.

4.—I put off kumn when she hollrd ferst.

5.—I put off maikn spead aftr arrivn at the sean uv distress.

6.—An werst uv awl, I wair on the levvl with an automobeel theef an a bank bandit bekawz I laft.

I tride 2 ecksplain to her how fearfl funny she lookt, but the moar I ecksplaind the maddr she got.

Its jest like yoo sed, Mistr Editr, wimmn aint got no sents uv yoomr.

Yoars, the goat, az yoozhl,

BEN PUTTIN-IT-OFF

TALL CORN? WELL I GUESS SO—.

Dear Editors: We, two people of Stephenson County, Illinois, in order to protect the interests of our cheese manufacturers and to preserve the natural beauty of the moon for the unmarried, do post this letter, trusting that the readers of the Farm Life will cooperate with us in our honest endeavor for justice.

Peter Brick, a farmer in this vinicity who is noted for his tall corn, is the person whom we accuse of being the cause of the following disturbance.

On a calm night two weeks ago, while passing Mr. Brick's residence on our way home from a late show, we were startled by a loud thud, and instantly the air was filled with fine, yellow, dust-like particles making it difficult for us to breathe and impossible to see. One storm followed another until the wheels spun in the yellow powder and we were unable to move on.

We alighted from the car and started walking to Mr. Brick's home for help. Upon nearing the place, we saw a huge, somewhat luminous object fall almost directly in front of us, and there followed a terrific dust storm. The remainder of that night and succeeding nights, we watched the movements of our neighbor. In this way, having discovered his secret, we feel that we can justly testify against him.

This is his secret: About four o'clock in the afternoon he plants a kernel of corn and immediately it starts to grow. With a parachute tied to his back, he clings desperately to the top of the stalk as it shoots upward. Before long, he is out of sight. Then he shakes the pollen from the tassel until there is a deep bed about the monstrous stalk. Before long a large slab of green cheese falls, which he slashed off the moon (for everyone knows the moon is made of green cheese.) The impact of the cheese in the pollen causes the storms of dust. Near sunrise, after alighting with his parachute, he stores the cheese away and blows up the stalk with dynamite. This process, he goes through almost every night. We conclude that as soon as the cheese is ripe, he will put it on the market.

I know you will cooperate with us and refuse to buy any of Brick's brick cheese. Yours for justice, —Youd B. Sprized, Ill.

But Bring Telescopes

Dear Editors: I always looked for a North Dakota man on the tall corn page, but our people are too modest. I was blown off my feet when I saw a Minnesota man boast one big wheat crop. I felt ashamed for the whole state of N. Dak. No, this is not going to be another tall corn story a'tall. But we are just finishing the biggest elevator in the world. We have been quite handicapped for water, as we pumped the Missouri river dry, and could work only every other day, waiting one day for it to fill. The elevator is built of solid concrete. It is big enough to store all the wheat from North Dakota and Montana and plenty room left for all the Tall Corn you fellows are going to raise in the future. But I warn you, you will have to bring a telescope with you, to find your grain.

Would you two fellows from Missouri and Washington, who had the corn stalks dropped across the Missouri and Columbia river please send me your address? A friend would like to have those cornstalks for pipe stems. —John Esa, N. Dak.

The prosecuting attorney levelled a long finger at the lanky witness from Basswood Hollow and yelled: "Did I understand you to say the witness was shot midway between the diaphram and the duodenum?" "No you didn't nuther," the witness declared. "I said he was shot 'bout half way b'tween the hog pen an' the wood shed!"

"Is this milk pasteurized?"
"I guess so. I bought the cow from a preacher."

. . . Aunt Hannah Beasley, who talked at the Woman's Club

last Friday, sez she has had so many inquiries about the word "Gullup" she used in tellin' how to make molasses cookies, she wants me to explain over the air. A gullup—When you turn up a jug of molasses, and as it pours out the molasses says "Gullup," and for one batch of cookies you use three gullups of molasses.

A Country Agent's Troubles
*Some Are Too Young, Says Mr. O'Riley
and Then There's "th' Ixecutiv' Comity"*
By W. Milton Kelly

Leaving his team to rest for a moment, Mr. Schwartz came over to the fence where Mr. O'Riley met him for a little talk.

"Iss der new county agent come yet?" Mr. Schwartz asked. "I hope der committee treats him better as they did Jansen. He vas a goot man for der job."

"Jansen was too practhical a farmer," said Mr. O'Riley, "Whiniver he thried to do anny-thing fr' th' farmer th' comity called a spechil meetin' an' ray-solved to sandbag him. Iveryboody tuk a crack at him whin th' Co-ops bustid."

"Vell der committee should be happy," said Mr. Schwartz "dey vanted some von better as Jansen. I vonder does dis new one drive der autobeel."

"He's an ixpirt dhriver," said Mr. O'Riley, "ye can mark th' pro-gress iv' th' la'ad be th' dead chickens an' dooks an' dawgs, an' th' wrecks iv' wag-gons an' autobeels along th' roads. He's a good man, though young as most iv thim are. He's twinty-four."

'Tis a gr-reat wur-ruld. Youth must be sarved. 'Tis old men f'r farmers an' young men f'r advice. Sum day whin we hobble up to th' Coort House to submit a gr-reat question iv organization, th' county agent will be sittin' in a high chair at th' desk suckin' a lolly-pop an' screamin' f'r ice crame."

"Mind ye, I am sthrong f'r th' county agent as an institoochin. He can help th' farmer kape out iv th' way iv manny troubles iv th' business. I ray-mimber th' first time Jansen dhrove to me farm to vaccinate me pigs. 'Twas a gr-reat thing f'r th' pigs and ivry wan liv-ved. He had two bhottles iv ser-rum; one ful iv virros ser-rum of dishease germs, an' th' other full of protective ser-rum, or innimies iv th' dishease.

Just Like Politics

"He gav' thim a hyper-dermick iv wan, an' thin wan iv th' other. He ixplained to me how th' vir-rus germs or th' dimmy-crats, stharted th' dishease in th' pig's systim; an' how th' good ol' protictiv' germs, or raypublicans, ate up th' little dim-mycrats an' massacreed thim, so th't th' pig's siveral rods iv circulatoory systim an' intestines were turned into a veritable civil up-risin' an' how the sthruggle wint on till th' dimmycrats was sub-jooed.

"Th' first year I came to th' counthry Jansen dhrove to me farm and showed me how to thrate me seed oats f'r smut an' rust, an' th' kind of phossy-phate to use f'r me crops, an' what to mix wit' th' manure to doub-ble its value. Befure he dhrove out I spint a long time thrying to figger out me farmin' systim, but wit' his help 'twas aisy. He made a map iv th' farm an' give me a lot ov pints on plannin' me rhotations. Ye see, Schwartz, a city business man, whin he begins in th' counthry, is a busi-ness man, an' that's all he is."

"I takes three years to make a farmer out iv him, n'l man-ny times think a little longer, if he is a good business man an' don't go broke in th' mane time. If he lives a very simple pasth-orial life, an' is popularly known as Cy, he may hang on f'r a long time. That's th' raison I sign me name Cyrus insthead iv Cornelius O'Riley. 'Tis a better name f'r a farmer.

A Name Worth Money

"A lot of la'ads whose names are Cy don't appracyate th' ad-vertisin value iv th' name. I've got sum aig custhomers in th' city what'll pay tin cints a doz-zen more f'r aigs f'r th' previlage iv callin' me Cy. An' since th' Co-ops wint busted I have to sell me pro-jooce to th' privhate thrade.

"In-dade Jansen was wan dacint county agent, an' ex-thraordinary wan, an' agreeable wan, an' always willin' to show ye what to do. 'Twas a shame he iver fell into th' hands iv th' ixecutiv' comity iv th' farm burrue; who bein' ach-ootated be a common purpose, after makin' a fizzel iv th' co-operatin' business, made him th' goat."

" 'Twas th' introdooctin iv co-operatin in th' fair counthry that marked th' beginnin' iv his end. Whin ye see an ixecutiv' comity iv a farm burrue th't ray-simbles a bunch iv wise ol' la'ads wit' long whiskers playin' siven-up, 'tis a bad sign f'r th' poore county agent."

"Chass! der executive committee iss on der blink," said Mr. Schwartz, "der old boirds gif me der pain. It iss no vonder der bisness went on der bummer. Ve should right away get busy next month and elect some new vons."

Be yourself if other folk can put up with it.

"ESSAY ON GEESE"

A geese is a low heavy set bird with mostly meat and feathers. His head sits on one end and his feet on the other. He ain't got no cracks between his toes, and he's got a big balloon on his stomach to keep him from sinkin'. Some geese when they gits big has curls on their tails, and is called ganders. Ganders don't haf to set and hatch, but just eat and loaf an go swimmin'. If I was a geese I'd rather be a gander.

The Troubles of
Poor Ben Puttin-It-Off

He Has a Patent Potato Digger

Deer Editr—I wair Fridy g.m. I wair in the prtaitr patsh bak uv the barn: Ebneezr and Bingo and Snap wair thair, too.

"Sikm, Neezr," I hollrz. "Wrats, Bingo; ketchm, boy." I slapt my hanz and eggdm on to dig in the spots Ide pintd out.

Purty soon thay wair awl werkn bootifly, and I sat doun in the shaid to rest. By wissln and hollrn nown then I kep the dogz bizzy on the job.

It wair about hear that Marthy appeard on the sean.

"Ben Puttin-It-Off," sez she, "its a wundr that I aint ben in the insain asilm long ago."

"Yes," sezzi, to agrea with her.

"Hear," sez she, "I send yoo out to dig prtaitrz, an find yoo fooln away yoar time with a pak uv werthls kurz."

"Lemme xplain," sezzi. But she grabd up the ho Ide brung along and not yoozd, an waivd it vilntly b4 me.

"Ive a noshn to braik this oavr yoor mpty pait."

"Woomn," sezzi, steppn outa rainj uv the ho hanl. "Didja evvr heer uva fellr naimd Ike Walton? An appl fel on him an giv him an idee. He run fr kongress an past the law uv gravitaishn."

"Whass that got too doo with diggn theaze prtaitrz?" sez she.

"Evrything, woomn," sezzi. "Wen I get theaze dogs traind to digm and putm in the baskt, Ile get me sicks uthr dogs and taik kontracks. Ile be maikn a washtub fulla munny," sezzi.

"Yoor a blithrn, bo-laigd idjit," sez she, an then a klod uv durt hit me in the mouth. She sez she wair thrown at the dogz, but Ime not sertn.

"Thass yoo," sezzi, fewrsly, az she begin pickn up prtaitrz an puttn them in the baskt. "Evrytime I get a big idee yoo kum along an bust it awl up. I rekn yoo doant no," sezzi, "that I wair aimn to by yoo a pair uv pink silk stocknz an sum bloo dimnd beadz with summa the munny I maid outa my grait diskuvry. I le put that off a long time, yoo bet," sezzi.

Yoarz in diskurjmnt,

BEN PUTTIN-IT-OFF.

P. S. —Marthy sez she nevvr see a patnt dog, but I tellr a fellr seaz a lotta thingz theaz daiz he nevvr sean be4.

Hoss shoes are good luck . . . if on the winning horse.

Not only corn grows big! Nosireebob!

Editors Farm Life: Well sir, it were two years ago that an impressive young feller come along and talked Pap into buying some beans. Well, Pap thought he would try a coupla bushels and sich beans you never seed. Them there beans grew so people thot we had set out a wood-lot. Well it came harvest time and we sawed off the pods and hauled them up to the barn, three at a time on a wagon, and it took six fellers with wedges and sledge hammers to crack them open and get the beans out. Four beans filled a hundred pound bag.

We sold the leaves to a paper concern for builders paper, and then we sawed down the vines, which were five feet through, and cut them into lumber. It took Pap and me all spring to get the stumps pulled out so we could plant beans again. Oh yes, I forgot to mention that we took the pods and slapped a couple coats of paint on them, and sold to a summer resort for canoes.

What's that? No, we only saved enough seed for ourselves. Hoping this don't sound exaggerated, I remain, yours for better beans. —Truman E. Smith, Mich.

A feller ought always to be ready for tomorrow but it's a heckuva mistake to count on it.

On Doddering

Grandpa doddered yesterday for the first time!

We children noticed it and laughed in glee and clapped our hands.

"Oh grandpa," we cried, "you doddered! Do it again!"

Then we ran to the neighbors and told them to come over and see Grandpa dodder.

"Dodder for them, Grandpa!" we pleaded.

And he did it.

Grandpa had an uncle who used to hold the doddering open championship. Everywhere they held a dodderfest Grandpa's uncle went and doddered. It got so that if the others knew Grandpa's uncle was going to dodder, the others would cancel their entries and not dodder against him. He outdoddered every person that ever tried to outdodder him. Every years between the dates of the leading dodder contests the others would just practice and practice doddering, hoping to get at least one decision over Grandpa's uncle, but each year Grandpa's uncle had the advantage of another year on them and he would dodder better than ever. He was sent to England to take part in the great international doddering regatta, and he won hands down, bringing home the cup the very first time he entered. And there were people there who doddered in all languages. By winning it three times in succession he managed to keep the cup for his very own.

Finally he was prevailed upon to open a dodder school and give lessons in plain and fancy doddering, to people who were above seventy. Soon his school was so crowded he had to start two or three night classes. After that only Grandpa's uncle and those who had been his pupils or pupils of his graduates were considered real dodderers.

Grandpa says one sees very little good doddering nowadays.

Buggin' Taters

Of late years I have trekked over the B. & A. through Aroostook country, Maine, and watched the horsedrawn spraying machines squirt their bugbane on the tater-trees. Those fellows at that lazy job looked persecuted-like and apparently thought they were working!

Huh! Those fellows hadn't been nowhere nor seen nothin'.

I used to bug taters, personally. I gave my undivided attention to each bug, hard or soft, and to each batch of eggs, and I know whereof I wail.

I used to take an old tin pail and a stick. With the latter I'd knock the bugs into the former, and carry them to some convenient place to pour scalding and death-dealing water on them.

But that process was scientific and easy, compared with the cruder methods used earlier.

I have spent many an hour with my spinal column curved like a rainbow, turning up potato-plant leaves to find the little clusters of yellow eggs and crushing them between two flat pieces of wood or stone.

Then the tiny, tender, soft-shelled fellows of assorted sizes! They were invariably in robust health.

I never saw a "dauncy" potato bug in my life. Whatever infant mortality there was to be, I arranged for. They squashed lovely.

Of course when we found one of the old striped hardshelled beetles (Colorado bugs we called 'em) himself, we had to be careful, or he'd let loose and play possum and drop down among the leaves and clods and be harder to find than a Republican voter in Texas. —Strickland Gillilan.

... Treatee Jones sez he is goin', to reverse his plantin' this spring by puttin' in weed seed to see if corn comes up.

FISH STORIES

In the fields of heaven in a quiet nook Noah and Ike Walton
   and Jonah found a brook,
Where the trout were teeming, where the grass was green
And the willows nodded in their silver sheen;
Laughter in the eyes of them, sunshine in their hair,
Old men who were dreaming, they just settled there;
As they baited silver hooks from a golden pail,
Jonah chuckled, "I'm the chap was swallowed by the
   whale!"
Noah made the first cast where the ripples ran;
As he played his gleaming prize, he was saying, "Man,
Whenever I am fishing it's bringing back to me
The time I clamped the hatches down and started out to
   sea.
Fishing? That was fishing, I am telling you;
I would open up a port—the fish would jump right through!
Never saw the likes of it since I took that sail."
Jonah muttered, "I'm the chap was swallowed by the
   whale!"

Noah's catch eluded him; Walton calmly took

A grasping, struggling beauty from his dripping hook,
Then he drawled, "It seems as though it happened yester-
    day—
Oh, how sweet the fragrance of the snowy hawthorne
    spray!—
I dropped my hook in rapture into the river Tyne,"
He yawned, "I hauled it out and lo, six fishes held my line!"
Jonah pulled his catch in, hearkening the tale,
Then he spat and snorted, "I was swallowed by the whale!"
                                    —Edgar Daniel Kramer.

The ringdoves mourn
    In tones forlorn,
Till I can scarce suppress a tear.
Their taxes too
    Must all fall due
About this season of the year!

The Troubles of Poor Ben Puttin-It-Off
—He Works a Miracle

Deer Editr—I wair sittn on a log in the barn lot wishn I had
a rich unkl, when the red roastr stopt and the strainjr jined me.

He wair a frendly fellr, Ed Hoaldm by naim, and he wunst
wair a poar farmer himself.

"Now," sezzee, givn me a good seegar, "Ime maikn gobs uv
munny, and livn on Eazy streat."

"I wisht I noo yoar seakrt," sezzi.

"Nobuddyl evvr no it but myself," sezzee. "It's a farmyoolay
that maix gold, pure gold, reel gold, frum wattr."

"Wattr? Gold frum wattr?"

"Nuthn moar, Ben. A foo draps uv this majikl kompound ex-
trax the oxide uv hydrospoofus and kombinez it with the exit
uv nitrospondoolix, maikn smal flaix uv gold."

"For kats saix," sezzi, "have yoo got enny uv this stuff with
yoo?"

Fer ansr he pulz frum hiz pokt a bottl about the size uv my
fingr, with sum pink stuff in it.

"Wanta sea how it werx, Ben? Kum on oavr to the hoss troff."

He hung hiz koat on the fents an we went oavr to the troff, Ed hoaldn the littl bottl uv Wundrgolda in his hand.

"Yood bettr pump sum fresh wattr in the troff, wun buckt, ennyway," sez zee," and while I follrd instrukshns he stood idly dabbln wun hand in the wattr alreddy in the troff.

"Now weal werk the modrn meerakl," sezzee, sprinkln a few draps intoo the troff. "Weal hafta wait about ten minits fer the kemikl inakshn to taik plaice."

We set on the logz, while he toald me sum funny stoariez about his travvlz, and then went bak to the troff.

Thair, floatn around the wttr wair the goldn flaix, jest as he sed.

"How mutch?" sezzi.

But Ed Hoaldm jest laft.

"Why shood I sell it?" he axd. "I doant nead enny munny. I kin taik this littl vile uv Wundrgolda and extrak $825 werth uv verjn gold frum a foo troffs full uv wattr."

"How mutch duz wunna thoaze bottlz kost yoo?"

"About twenty dollrz," sezzee. "Wel, I gotta bee goin."

"Wait a minnit, Ed." sezzi, figgrn rapidly.

Thair wair fiftean dollrz left uv the koalt munny whitch Marthy wair to pay Kinzy on the stoar bill, and foar or five dollarz uv the egg munny in the kitchn saif.

Lucky fer mee Marthy wair at the Laidiez Aide.

I pled with Mr. Hoaldm fer a while, and he finely giv up.

"Well, why not, Ben?" sezzee. "Git yoar twenty. I doant mind dooin yoo a faivr."

It wair not moarn three minits aftr the transakshn wair kompleated and the red roadstr roard away, when Marthy kaim hoam.

I wair jest reddy to spring my happy serprize, when she sed:

"I herd sumthn funny at the Ade, today. An I dunno az yood kall it funny, eathr. A slik sitty fellrz ben around selln sumthn thatll tern wattr intoo gold, and he got twenty dollrz frum Ab Wix. Thay went to the spring, and while Ab wairnt notisn the raskl doaps the wattr with hiz Wundrgolda stuff."

"Howd thay no the fellr waz a faik?" sezzi.

"Alik Wiggns ketchdim rite in the act, Ben. He dropt in a kap-shool uv this stuff thay mix goald paint with, while Ab wairnt lookn. Ab aint enny too brite, ennyway. He giv that skoundrl $20 uv his tax munny."

"I feal sorry fer Liddy," she goez on, "havn to live with a man that iz not oanly laizy, but that aint got enny sents at all."

"Mee too," sezzi, feably, tappn wunna my vest pokts to sea if that bottl wair still thair.

"Whass the mattr, Ben?" sez she. "Yoo aint eatn enny suppr."

'I aint fealn so wel," sezzi, pushn away frum the taibl.

No mam, Marthy aint found yet whair the munny went.

Yes mam, Ime puttn off the konfeshn az long as possibl. But sheal maik me tellr, yet.

Sadly yoarz,

BEN PUTTIN-IT-OFF

Nowadays when you tell a girl that you'd go through any-thing for her, she wants to know how much you've got to go through.

. . . All the good advice in the world can be drowned out by the rustle of a woman's skirt.

Same Old Story

We get sad news of a coming end
From our returned globe-trotters:
They say "we've gone too far to mend—
All civilization totters!"

'Twas Adam coined that phrase; said he,
"A terrible pair of plotters
Old Satan and the serpent be—
And civilization totters."

And Noah voiced the self-same fear
When his ark rode the waters;

He sighed and said, as he dropped a tear,
"This civilization totters."

"What, what'll I do?" So King Tut cried,
(He was one of our first what-what-ers)
"Go make me a tomb, and let me hide—
For civilization totters."

Yet good still governs the world today
And man stands on his trotters;
So let's take heart and be on our way—
Though civilization totters.

Deacon Hornblower heard that the apple crop was likely to be a water-haul that year, because of threatened invasions by pests. To the other apple growers assembled he said solemnly, as he started to kneel down:
"Let us pray."
But Ike Hardboyle took his hat and started out of the room saying:
"Let us spray."
Moral: Faith without works is dead.

"Talk about having inflammatory rheumatism and St. Vitus dance," said the thoughtful man. "But what about having lockjaw and seasickness?"

Song of the Flivver
By Blaine C. Bigler

I go to haunts for which you yearn;
I make a sudden sally;
I rattle, shiver, twist and turn;
I bicker down the valley.

I run, I glide, I bump, I jump;
I miss, backfire and quiver;
I overheat and skid and pump;
I shake your heart and liver.

I rattle underneath the stars;
  I rumble on the bridges;
I squeak at many little jars;
  I grind o'er sundry ridges.

I tremble when I go to stop;
  I tremble when I'm running;
I tremble til I lose my top
  And then you get a sunning.

I am the flivver, don't you know?
  My way's not smooth—no never.
But cars may come and cars may go
  Yet I go on forever.

Th' Wife on th' Farm
by Abe Martin

I don't think woman wuz ever cut out fer farm work, an' I think th' headstones in Tharps Run cemetery 'll bear me out.

She hain't muscled fer it, an' her instincts are finer than a male's, and not adopted t' hog raisin', grubbin' an' manure spreadin'.

Splittin' wood an' plowin' destroy a woman's natural contour.

Foolin' with chickens, an' even a little modest churnin', are harmless diversions that may not enhance feminine beauty, or stimulate woman's intellectual qualities, but they do no particular harm.

However, on th' modern, well equipped farm, drudgery has been practically eliminated, an' ther remains little t' do that kin be said t' retard th' intellectual advancement, or warp th' frame o' the' farmer's wife.

Agriculture has advanced considerable.

I kin remember when a farmer picked out a wife jest like he picked out a work horse.

He'd walk around her two or three times an' size her up.

Mebbe he'd pinch her arms, or look at her teeth, or trot her back an' forth a few times, an' then listen t' her breathin'.

He wuz lookin' fer a partner that could grub some new land, or ditch a meadow, or do some loggin'.

Pickin' out a wife fer farm work wuz a purely business proposition, an' ther wuz' no sentiment mixed up in it.

Th' ole time farmer wanted a good, sound draft wife, one that wuz gentle an' ploddin' an' wouldn' scare—a woman anybuddy could drive.

Lon Moon's father wore out four wives before he got his farm in good shape. His fifth wife got scared an' ran off th' day he started t' blow th' stumps in th' field next t' th' Bently farm. He wrote t' her an' promised t' put a pump in th' kitchen if she'd come back, but he never heard from her.

———————

"Bury me with a hog," said the old farmer, as he flickered his eyes open for the last time. "I've never been in a tight place yet but my hogs pulled me out."

———————

Having been caught with some cattle he could not account for, the defendant had entered a plea of guilty; and had thrown himself on the mercy of the court.

"Have you anything to say before I pass sentence?" inquired the judge.

"Well," offered the defendant, after a moment's deliberation, "I always closed the pasture gate after me."

———————

The Modern Mode

The short skirt maid, and the sheer waist maid
    They strut their stuff today,
And year after year, the girlies dear
    Keep throwing their clothes away.

Oh, where is the maid of grandma's time?
    And where is the fleecy shawl?
Girl's clothes get thinner and fewer—what
    Will be the end of it all?

But when I look at the modern maid
Go rollicking down the way
I can't help but think the style will end
With the old fig leaf some day.

Jack H. Smith

And a similar cut of cloth:

It used to be said that a man was pretty small who would hide behind his wife's skirts. These days he'd have to be a dwarf and use stilts.

Some women are like wine, they improve with age; others are like cider, age makes them turn to vinegar. The man who questions whether he is married to wine or vinegar might present his wife with a pound box of good candy. A little sweetening improves even wine, I am told, and it will cover a lot of sour in vinegar.

This reminds me of a man I learned of last week. His wife had long been neglected so, after hearing all such actions properly lined up by a lecturer one afternoon, he bought a box of candy, took it home and presented it to his wife.

She burst into tears and dropped down into a chair. "What's the matter?" he asked in the endearing tones of years before.

"Everything has gone wrong today," she sobbed. "First the house caught on fire, then Johnny fell down and broke his arm and now you've come home drunk."

Scientists have found out how to make 146 different things from corn. What the middle west now wants is a dependable way to make profits from it.

Figs and Thistles
Gathered by O. G. Whizz

Ah, March, we know thou art
Kind-hearted spite of ugly looks and threats,
And, out of sight, art nursing April's violets.

—Helen Hunt Jackson

It is high time that something was done about the weather. However else we are harpooned, the weather remains our chief problem. We sow and know not whether we shall reap a price-wrecking yield, or barely enough to pay for our binder twine and chewing tobacco. Beef herds perish in blizzards, the hogs drown in spring floods, and cyclones abolish our houses and barns. Between these and divers other wallops we almost come, in darker moments, to wish with Mark Twain that Noah had missed the boat.

But what to do—aye mates, there looms the question. Its answer seemed to devolve on this department. No one, not even Congress in the leanest years of bait for votes, has ever even hinted that anything could be done about the weather. This neglect shall now be repaired, for I reveal a balm in Gilead, and unfold a plan ov vast excellence, a plan that—but you shall judge for yourselves.

The bright, beautiful remedy is simply this: Make the weather bureau at Washington responsible for the weather's pranks and depravities. Naturally enough, you recoil a bit and ahem somewhat at first—so unused are folks to pure unwatered sense in public affairs. But, brethren, reflect. Here is an institution with sole charge of the weather—we plant our pumpkins, cut our alfalfa and arrange our picnics according to its prognostications. When the Bureau deceives us should it not repay our losses? Certainly it should.

Where will the money be got? The answer, fellow horseshoe throwers, will delight your perplexed hearts. Turn for an instant to the verse at the top of this column. Millions, if not billions, of such sweet sugary things are annually rhymed about the weather. It is the chief topic with poets. Take the weather away from them, and I suppose that all the poetry about every other subject from women to whippoorwills, would dwindle to a few thousand car loads a year.

Here then, we have a huge source of revenue ready to be tapped. Let Congress authorize the Weather Bureau to license the use of weather in poetry, and severely chastise its merest mention by a poet having no license. Automobiles are licensed, as also is doctoring, peddling, running restaurants, and trapping skunks. Why should poeting be an exception anyhow?

A glance through the public prints must convince you that the proceeds of an annual fee of say $100 per poet would give the Weather Bureau huge bins of cash from which to square up for its mistakes. There would, of course, be loud squawks of anguish from the poets, but Progress always barks some shins in its onward drive. Besides, poets erupt many of their niftiest rhymes when deeply panged, so that this scheme would really be for their best good. It is no less perfect than that.

You will agree with me, genial readers, that action cannot be taken too soon. It is not only that the need is sore, but Congress may hop onto so promising a source of revenue as that poet-license stuff any day. We must be up and doing, before the finances for our achievement are perhaps diverted to a broom corn bureau or a commission to feed cough drops to hoarse bull frogs.

Si Skinner clasped his hands together so tight durin' prayer time at church yestiddy that he couldn't git 'em open when the planter was passed around.

Great Fortunes an' Farmin'
By Abe Martin

Somebuddy is allus dyin' an leavin' a great fortune, but they've allus been engaged in some business other than farmin'.

We read ther biographies—ther early hardships on th' farm, how they tore out an' got int' other business, how they struggled an' held on until they got on a payin' basis.

Men have amassed great fortunes in ever' blamed business but farmin'.

How'd it sound t' read, "Jake Bently Leaves Millions t' Art Museum. Many Other Bequests. Started as Poor Boy in

Great Industrial Center, an' by Hard Work an' Frugal Habits, Becomes a Farmer at th' Age o' Thirty-one. Dies Commandin' Figure in th' Field o' Agriculture?"

Th' farm seems t' be th' school o' hard knocks that qualify a feller t' clean up in other walks o' life.

Ther's no reason, since we're all protected by th' same tariff wall, why agriculture shouldn' produce a great public benefactor once in awhile, some big successful sheep raiser, or corn grower, or hog wizard, or p'tater czar, t' help along art museums an' things.

Besides turnin' out th' foodstuffs of a nation th' farm seems t' specialize on turnin' out business wizards.

If it wuzn' fer th' early, rugged life on th' farm, I doubt if a great art museum would be possible, t' say nothin' o' many other great institutions.

Frank A. Munsey, who died recently, wuz born on a Maine farm, an' got his groundin' in th' first principles o' life from th' curriculum o' good, hard work that is th' common lot o' th' farm-bred boy.

Then he struck out an' finally owned a half dozen great metropolitan newspapers.

It took several days t' find out how many millions he'd made since givin' up agriculture.

———————

. . . When a feller that's mad at you calls you a name, you'd better look it up and see if he ain't right.

———————

. . . If hard luck drives a feller to drink, you know dern well that prosperity would have killed him!

———————

Advice on the proper way
to eat sweetcorn.

For many a year there has been a dire need for instruction on how to eat SWEETCORN ON THE COB. We hope the following erudite treatise will answer this need to the satisfaction of all red-blooded American trenchermen/women.

First off, there is no need at all to consider etiquette when one prepares to imbibe first-rate sweetcorn on the cob. There is simply no wisdom that refutes the ancient adage that good manners spoil good corn or, the reverse, that good corn requires no observance of good manners. The thing to do is to get down to the nut cuttin' and quit worrying about what the neighbors might say. Drop all the acquired habits of reserve, timidity, etiquette and neighborly considerations, and just . . . go . . . to . . . it. To heck with Emily Post.

Now that we have established the required *caveats*, let us get down to the kernel of the thing. You begin from the left and eat a complete swath to the right not pausing or otherwise wasting time. Once to the end, rotate slightly and eat your way, gourmetically, back. This non-stop method has gained many a knowledgeable corn eater seconds and thirds when there wasn't enough corn to go around the table. Mesmerize your conscience and your sense of fitness and think only of the corn (when among mixed and obviously avaricious table mates).

Advice of long standing holds that you must pay no attention to flying kernels or dripping butter or a missed kernel or two. Gnaw as fast as you can and don't stop to commiserate with your neighbor who is minus two front teeth (you can do that later). And remember that there will be plenty of time to wipe your buttery cheeks clean later, at which time you can dig stray kernels out of your ears, wipe your eyebrows clean and explore your nostrils for vagrants. Do all your cleaning up *after* the corn-bearing platter is empty.

If you practice the above technique daily for at least thirty days before sweet corn gets ripe, you will never get caught short when it comes to gorging yourself on the gourmet's *piece de resistance*.

When our laziest citizen, Pete Brown, was told by the manager of his boarding house that he had just three days to pay his bill for room and board, he chose Labor Day, Christmas Day and Fourth of July.

The way some fellows brag on their wives make a guy wonder if they really love 'em or want to sell 'em.

... Bill Spugs says the chinch bugs wuz so bad out his way he had to creosote his ankles to keep them from eatin' up his straw hat.

These seven jokes are from: COUNTRY GENTLEMAN–1916.

So He Was Happy

"You haven't had all that you wanted in life, now, have you?" asked the pessimist.

"No," replied the optimist, "but I haven't had all that I didn't want, either."

A colored preacher was vehement, denouncing the sins of his congregation. "Bredern an' sistern, Ah warns yo' 'gainst de heinous sin ob shootin' craps! Ah charges yo' 'gainst de black rascality ob liftin' pullets. But above else, bredern an' sistern, Ah demolishes yo' 'gainst de crime ob melon stealin'."

A brother in a back seat made an odd sound with his lips, rose and snapped his fingers. Then he sat down again with an abashed look.

"Whuffo, mah fren'," said the parson sternly, "does yo' rar up an' snap yo' fingahs when Ah speaks ob melon stealin'?"

"Yo' jes remin's me, pahson," the man in the back seat answered meekly, "wha' Ah lef' mah knife."

A farmer, on a trip to the city thought he would take home a shirtwaist as a present to his wife. In a department store he asked the clerk to show him some waists.

"What bust?" asked she.

Looking round quickly the farmer answered: "I don't know; I didn't hear nothing."

A convert, full of zeal, in his first prayer meeting offered himself for service. "I am ready to do anything the Lord asks of me," said he, "so long as it's honorable."

An exhorter in a negro camp meeting in Alabama had just made a great speech. When he got through he went down among the congregation and asked each one to join the army of the Lord.

One of the congregation, when this question was put to him, replied:

"I'se done jined."

"Whar'd you' jine?" asked the exhorter.

"In de Baptist church."

"Why, chile," said the exhorter, "yo' ain't in de army, yo's in de navy."

At the end of six weeks of married life a southerner returned to the minister who had performed the ceremony and asked for a divorce. After explaining that he could not give divorces the minister tried to dissuade his visitor from carrying out his intention.

"You must remember, Sam, that you took Liza for better or for worse."

"I knows that boss," rejoined the groom "but she's wuss than I took her fer."

. . . Bide Smith asked Uncle Hooper Green if he liked bananas. Uncle Hooper is hard of hear'n and answered, "No, I stick to old-fashioned night gowns."

No collection of farm and ranch stories would be complete without a Paul Bunyan tale. Sure he was a great lumberjack. But he was equally good at farming and ranching; and the following "history" is all the proof you need.

After Paul got the south side o' Mount' Hood all logged off, he hitched his Blue Ox to his heavy plow, the one that'd turn forty acres to two furrers, an' started in breakin' it fer plantin'. But he didn't git much done, fer Babe he stepped into a yeller-jacket's nest an' run away draggin' the plow 'long. The gash he made in the hills folks calls the Columbia River Gorge. Paul he never did colleck the pieces o' that thar plow.

Paul he tried his hand at ever'thin goin'—built a sky-scrapin' hotel wunst down here on the Big Trail. That thar wuz a hotel—spread over more'n ten acres, an' had the last seven stories put on hinges so's they c'd be swung back fer to let the moon go by. The dinin'-room wuz seven hundred foot long, an' the bell-hops all wore roller skates.

An' Paul tried ranchin', tho loggin' wuz more in his line. I guess ever'body's heard 'bout the hard luck he had in Kansas. Some crook sold him a farm an' the soil wuz so rich nobody ever dast plant anythin' on it. Paul he went out fer to look it over an' on the way he dropped a kernel o' corn; an' by the time he'd went a few steps that thar corn wuz knee-high. He run to the house fer to get Sweede Charlie to watch it grow, an' by the time they got back it wuz higher'n their heads. Paul he figgered to cut the top off an' stop it growin' so he sent Charlie up the stalk, but he couldn't git to the top; an' when he tried to slide down he couldn't neither, fer it growed faster'n he c'd slide. He liked to starved till Paul loaded up his shot-gun with doughnuts an' shot 'em up to him. Then 'long come the Gov'ment Inspector an' sez: 'Paul, y' got to git that corn-stalk down; it's drainin' the Mississippi River dry and' interferin' with navigation.' Fin'lly Paul he sent fer a couple o' rails 'bout a mile long an' knotted 'em together round the stalk by runnin' Babe round it, an the faster it growed the more it cut itself. Jist then 'long come a cyclone an' finished it.

Y'ever see that cleared spot—'bout a hundred acres—up the Mackenzie River? Wal, that thar wuz Paul's ranch. He cal'lated to raise wheat on't; so he built a tight board fence round it an' sowed it to wheat. It jist got started an' a big hail-storm come on an' beat it into the ground. So Paul he planted it over ag'in, an' as soon's it got 'bout ripe 'long come a herd o' elk an' jumped the fence an' milled round an' trompted it all out. Wal, sir, both o' them seedin's 'd took, an' the grain wuz so heavy it run clean over the second board o' the fence.

Paul had his worst luck when he went into the hog business in Eastern Oregon. An' it wuzn't his fault neither. His ranch wuz clean back in the mountains an' the' wuzn't no road cut. He jist got a nice start an' somethin' begun to take the hogs—fifteen, twenty a night—an' fin'lly the corn begun to go, too. Paul seen some bear tracks an' he follered 'em thirty mile to a cave in Box Canyon; an' thar he found his hogs all fattened an' killed, an' the corn all stored in ricks. Wal, the buildin' o' the road to haul the meat out after it wuz cured et up all the profit—an' then some.

'Bout this time Babe come to an ontimely end. Paul an' his family wuz aspendin' the week-end at the camp on the Skomackaway an' Babe wuz 'long. He got hungry fer hotcakes an' they didn't give him none. He kicked an' pawed the ground so furious that the wind it made blowed over the cook shanty. Then he made straight fer it an' et up all the cakes, an' then he got so greedy he swallered the stove an' died o' 'cute indigestion. They butchered him right thar an' salvaged the stove an' shipped the meat away in sixty boxcars; an' folks've complained o' tough beefsteak ever since.

Yeh, I heard 'bout Paul bein' in Panama an' helpin' with the Canal; an' some sez he run the Spruce Division fer the World War. I dunno; but he didn't take Babe, ner the Big Elk. I know that fer a fact. I tol' y' what become o' Babe, an' they got the Elk's jaw in the Condon Muzeem.

An' now I'm done yarnin'. Them wuz great ol' days.—Guess, I'll go on up the Mackenzie an' git m'self a job acookin'.

. . . Grandpa Smelters is gettin' kind'a absent-minded lately. He put a penny in the mail box, looked up at the town clock and sed, "Gosh, I lost four pounds."

Marthy Disappoints Him Again

Deer Editr: —I flung the Shaidsvil Bewgl doun on the poartsch flore.

"It ain't fare," I sez bitterly.

"What ain't?" axes Marthy, pickn up the paipr and lain it, folded, on top of her mendn baskt.

"Yew no Ezry Sapp, that werks in the postoffis," sezzi. "Well, the paipr sez he got ten $$ the uthr day for rightn foar verses for a soap advertizement. Aint that offl?" sezzi.

"What is thair offl about it?" axes Marthy.

"Why duz Ezry Sapp get ten $$ for foar verses roat wun day when the 248 trane was lait, while I hafto urn awl my munny by the respiraishn of my hibrow?" sezzi, "and get calluses on my hands," sezzi, "and stoan broozes on my heals?" sezzi.

"Look at me," sezzi, waukn acrost the poartsch and standn by Marthy's chare. "Aint I got as good a rite to ten $$ as Ezry Sapp?"

"Aint I as hansum?" sezzi, "if I oanly had the silk sherts and talkm poudr, and things to maik me pritty? Heer I rize erly and toil til the settn of the sun—well, whatcher laffn at?"

"O, nuthn," sez Marthy, goan on with her soin.

"Why," sezzi, waivn my hands ellikwently, and nockn her specks inter her lap, "shoodnt hav pye a Shivaree car, and wair pink silk sherts, and hav pue for brekfst? Why?" I demands.

"But yew no," sez she, settn her specks back into plaice. "Ez Sapp has got branes. He is reel smart."

I lookt atter with spishn, but she was fittn a patsch on the sleeve of my uthr shert, and seamd so peesfl, I desided she didn't reeleyes how her remark sounded.

"Shucks, ennyboddy can right potery," seezzi, "and st to show you know eezy it is, Ile right yew a peace."

It took me 2 or 3 daze to get it polisht up to perfeckshn nd then I startd to reed my pome to Marthy. Heer is the first verse:

"In the bewtifl, dewtifl munth of June, When the flours and berds air awl in blume,

And the grass is grean, and sky is blune—"

"That's poetickl licentiousness," sezzi, "to maik the rime rite," sezzi—

—"And the berds on the wing,
And the june bugs sing,
And the cows eet grass like evrything."

"Hows that?" sezzi. Thairs nine moar stanzys of it, all as good as that."

"Its wundrfl," sez Marthy. "Simply wundrfl. If yewl sharpn

the acks and cut up sum stoavewood, Ile let yew reed me
the rest of it, Ben."

But I waukt off in silent dignitty. Its offl for a poet to be tide to
a woomn like that. I caint stand mutsch moar of it.

Yoars, with a broozd and woondd hart,

BEN PUTTIN-IT-OFF.

P.S.—Mistr Editr, I'll send yew the rest of that pome if youl
send me ten $$ for it. —B. P.

The Stingiest Man

The tightest man I ever knew
Would never let himself look through
His specs, but always wore them low
Down on his nose. He did this so
He could look over them, no doubt,
Thus keeping them from wearing out.

"Hey mister, I got a good question for
you: How fast can you climb that pole?"

Acknowledgments and Permissions

Ace Reid Enterprises. Kathy Laurie. Kerrville, TX.

Copyright Office, Reference & Bibliography Section. Mike Peterson. Washington, D.C.

Country. Roy Reiman, Publisher and Bob Ottum, Editor, Greendale, WI

Illinois Farm Bureau Library. Vince Sampson, Librarian. Bloomington, IL.

Illinois Historic Preservation Agency. Tom Schwartz. Springfield, IL.

The Little House Out Back. George Borum. Taylor Printing Co., Olney, IL.

Outhouse Humor. Billy Edd Wheeler. August House/Little Rock Publishers. Little Rock, AR.

A Penny's Worth of Minced Ham. Rev. Robert J. Hastings. Southern Illinois University Press. Carbondale and Edwardsville, IL.

Reggie the Retiree Co. Wesley N. Haines. Fort Myers, FL.

T. Perry Wesley. Spencer, IN.

Western Words: A Dictionary of the Range, Cow Camp and Trail, by Ramon F. Adams. Copyright © 1944 by the University of Oklahoma Press.

We are indebted to the Lincoln Library and the Illinois State Library of Springfield, Illinois, both for their Reference and Inter-Library Loan Departments. Most helpful has been Sondra Hastings, Inter-Library Loan Department, Illinois State Library, Springfield, Illinois.

Bibliography

Abe Lincoln Laughing. P.M. Zall, Ed. University of California Press. 1982.

A Corral Full of Stories. Joe M. Evans. The McMath Co., Inc. El Paso, Texas. 1939.

Anything For A Laugh. Bennett Cerf, Ed. Bantam Books. New York. 1946.

Bible in Pocket, Gun in Hand. Ross Phares. University of Nebraska Press. Lincoln, NE. 1977.

The Catholic Treasury of Wit and Humor. Paul Bussard, Ed. Hawthorne Books. 1966.

Charley Weaver's Letters From Mamma. Cliff Arquette. The John C. Winston Co. Philadelphia, PA 1959.

The Checker Playing Hound Dog. Joe Hayes. Mariposa Publicaitons. Santa Fe., N.M. 1986.

Collier's Collects Its Wits, Gurney Williams, Ed. Harcourt, Brace and Company. New York. 1941.

The Complete Army-Navy Joke Book. Bill Brower. Stravon Publishers. New York. 1952.

"Cullud" Fun. Jack Dionne. Rein Co. Houston, TX. 1932.

Encyclopedia of Black Folklore and Humor. Henry D. Spalding. Jonathon David Publishers. Middle Village, N.Y. 1972.

Folk Laughter on the American Frontier. Mody C. Boatright. The Macmillan Co. New York. 1949.

Four Hundred Good Stories. Robert Rudd Whiting. The Baker & Taylor Co. New York. 1910.

Fun & Laughter. The Reader's Digest Association, Inc. Pleasantville, NY. 1988.

1001 Great Jokes. Jeff Rover. Signet Books. 1987.

How'dy Ev'vybuddy! Uncle Ezra Watter. Magill-Weinsheimer. Chicago, IL. 1936.

Humorous Recitations and Stories. W. Foushan & Co., Ltd. Great Britain. 1953.

Humorous Tales of Latter Day Rabbis. Solomon M. Neches, D.H.L. George Dobsevage. New York. 1938.

I Give You Texas! Boyce House. The Naylor Co. San Antonio, TX. 1949.

It's A Funny World. Gurney Williams, Ed. Robert M. McBridge & Co. New York. 1943.

The Jewish Joke Book. Michael Dines. Futura Publications. London, England. 1986.

Jokes From Israel. Paul Hirschhorn. "Semana". Jerusalem, Israel. 1984.

Joke Tellers Joke Book. Frederick Meier. The Blakiston Co. Philadelphia, PA. 1944.

Ladies Choice. Mavis Patterson, Ed.. Thorndike Press. Thorndike, Miane. 1982.

Laugh Day. Bennett Cerf. Doubleday & Co., Inc. Garden City, N.Y. 1965.

The Laugh's On Me. Bennett Cerf. Doubleday & Company, Inc. Garden City. N.Y. 1959.

Laughing On The Outside. Philip Sterling, Ed. Grossett & Dunlap Publishers. New York. 1965.

Laughsville U.S.A. Scholastic Book Service. New York. 1965.

Library of Humor. Walter Buescher. Prentice-Hall, Inc. Englewood Cliffs, N.J. 1984.

The Life Of The Party. Bennett Cerf. Doubleday & Co., Inc. Garden City, N.Y. 1956.

Like We Say Back Home. Dick Syatt. Citadel Press. Secaucus, N.J. 1987.

Many Laughs For Many Days. Irvin S. Cobb. Garden City Publishing Co., Inc. Garden City, N.Y. 1925.

The Modern Handbook of Humor. Ralph L. Woods. McGraw-Hill Book Co. 1967.

Outhouse Humor. Billy Edd Wheeler. August House/Little Rock Publishers. Little Rock, AR. 1988.

Out of the Rock. Frank Dobie. Little, Brown & Co. New York, N.Y. 1955.

Phyllis Diller's Marriage Manual. Phyllis Diller. Fawcett Publications, Inc. Greenwich, CT. 1967.

Podium Humor. James C. Hume. Harper & Row. New York. 1975.

The Pulpit Treasury of Wit and Humor. Israel H. Weisfeld. Prentice-Hall. New York. 1950.

The Second Indoor Bird Watcher's Manual. Helen Ferril & Ann Folsom. Duell, Sloan and Pearce. New York. 1951.

The Second Jewish Joke Book. Michael Dines. Futura Publications. London. 1987.

Snappy Stories That Preachers Tell. Rev. Paul E. Holdcraft, S.T.D. The Stockton Press. Baltimore, MD. 1932.

The Sound Of Laughter. Bennett Cerf. Doubleday & Company, Inc. Garden City, N.Y. 1979.

Did You Hear The One About. . . Soupy Sales. MacMillan Publishing Co. New York. 1987.

Sparks Of Laughter. Stewart Anderson. Intelligencer Printing Co. Lancaster, PA. 1926.

Stop or I'll Scream! Gurney Williams, Ed. Robert M. McBridge & Co. New York. 1945.

Stories to Make You Feel Better. Bennett Cerf. Random House. New York. 1972.

Tall Talk From Texas. Boyce House. The Naylor Co. San Antonio. TX. 1949.

Tar Heel Laughter. Richard Walser, Ed. The University of North Carolina Press. Chapel Hill, N.C. 1974.

Texas—Proud & Loud. Boyce House. The Naylor Co. San Antonio, TX. 1949.

Texas Yarns and Jokes. William Davis Gill. The Naylor Company. San Antonio, Texas. 1952.

Thesaurus of Anecdotes. Edmund Fuller, Ed. Crown Publishers. New York. 1942.

A Treasury of American Folk Humor. James N. Tidwell, Ed. Crown Publishers, Inc. New York. 1956.

The Treasury of Clean Country Jokes. Tal D. Bonham. Broadman. Broadman Press. Nashville, TN. 1986.

A Treasury of Reader's Digest Humor. The Digest Association, Inc. Pleasantville, N.Y. 1949.

Waiter There's a Fly In My Soup. Paul Dickson. Dell Publishing Co. New York. 1984.

What the Old-Timer Said. Allen R. Foley. The Stephen Greene Press. Brattleboro, Vermont. 1983.

Willie Walkette. Aubry Robison. Mt. Vernon, IN.

You Can't Unfry An Egg. Robert Pershall. Phoenix Publishing. Canaan, N.H. 1973.

"If that's his final word, I'm gonna
take my business elsewhere!"

"Paw, you'd better hurry . . . the kids are playin' with your
chain saw agin!"

Write Your Own Jokes